1942

1943

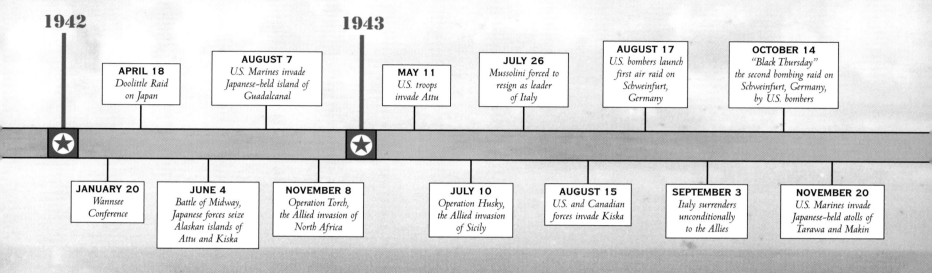

APRIL 18
*Doolittle Raid
on Japan*

AUGUST 7
*U.S. Marines invade
Japanese-held island of
Guadalcanal*

MAY 11
*U.S. troops
invade Attu*

JULY 26
*Mussolini forced to
resign as leader
of Italy*

AUGUST 17
*U.S. bombers launch
first air raid on
Schweinfurt,
Germany*

OCTOBER 14
*"Black Thursday"
the second bombing raid on
Schweinfurt, Germany,
by U.S. bombers*

JANUARY 20
*Wannsee
Conference*

JUNE 4
*Battle of Midway,
Japanese forces seize
Alaskan islands of
Attu and Kiska*

NOVEMBER 8
*Operation Torch,
the Allied invasion of
North Africa*

JULY 10
*Operation Husky,
the Allied invasion
of Sicily*

AUGUST 15
*U.S. and Canadian
forces invade Kiska*

SEPTEMBER 3
*Italy surrenders
unconditionally
to the Allies*

NOVEMBER 20
*U.S. Marines invade
Japanese-held atolls of
Tarawa and Makin*

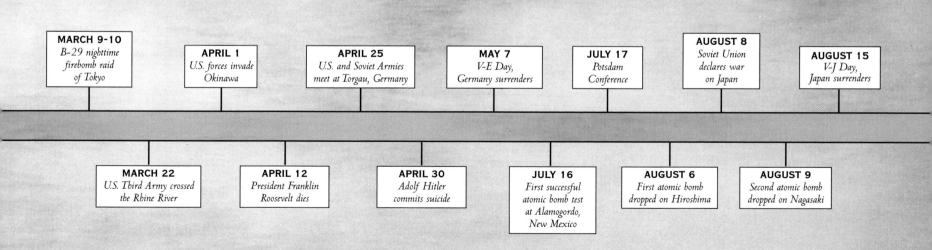

MARCH 9-10
*B-29 nighttime
firebomb raid
of Tokyo*

APRIL 1
*U.S. forces invade
Okinawa*

APRIL 25
*U.S. and Soviet Armies
meet at Torgau, Germany*

MAY 7
*V-E Day,
Germany surrenders*

JULY 17
*Potsdam
Conference*

AUGUST 8
*Soviet Union
declares war
on Japan*

AUGUST 15
*V-J Day,
Japan surrenders*

MARCH 22
*U.S. Third Army crossed
the Rhine River*

APRIL 12
*President Franklin
Roosevelt dies*

APRIL 30
*Adolf Hitler
commits suicide*

JULY 16
*First successful
atomic bomb test
at Alamogordo,
New Mexico*

AUGUST 6
*First atomic bomb
dropped on Hiroshima*

AUGUST 9
*Second atomic bomb
dropped on Nagasaki*

STEPHEN E. AMBROSE
THE GOOD FIGHT

HOW WORLD WAR II WAS WON

A Byron Preiss Visual Publications, Inc. Book

ATHENEUM BOOKS FOR YOUNG READERS
NEW YORK   LONDON   TORONTO   SYDNEY   SINGAPORE

To the grandchildren of the men and women who served in the U.S. armed forces in World War II.

Atheneum Books for Young Readers

An imprint of Simon & Schuster Children's Publishing Division

1230 Avenue of the Americas

New York, New York 10020

Front jacket photo caption: A soldier greets a mother and her child in France.

Title page photo caption (p. 1): An anti-aircraft gun battery on an unidentified aircraft
carrier fires at an approaching kamikaze plane.

Introduction page photo caption (p. 5): Soldiers in England taking a break during
a landing rehearsal for D-Day.

The text of this book is set in Monotype Centaur.

Printed in the United States of America

10 9 8 7 6 5 4 3

Library of Congress Cataloging-in-Publication Data

Ambrose, Stephen E.

The good fight / by Stephen E. Ambrose.

p.   cm.

Includes bibliographical references.

ISBN 0-689-84361-5

1. World War, 1939–1945—Juvenile literature. 2. World War, 1939–1945—United

States—Juvenile literature. [1. World War, 1939–1945. 2. World War, 1939–1945—

United States.] I. Title: The Good Fight. II. Title.

D743.7 .A43 2001

940.53—dc21   00-049600

FIRST
EDITION

★ PHOTO CREDITS

Anthony Potter Collection/Archive Photos: p. 21

AP/U.S. Signal Corps: p. 84 (top)

AP/Wide World Photo: pp. 57, 69, 70 (upper left), 72, and 74

Arnold Kramer/ U.S. Holocaust Memorial Museum: p. 68

Bettman/CORBIS: p. 85

Bundesarchiv: p. 22

CORBIS: p. 66

Defense Department/Marine Corps: p. 24

Eisenhower Center: p. 28

The Granger Collection, New York: pp. 13 and 83

Imperial War Museum: pp. 12, 78 (both photos), 80, and 81

Library of Congress: pp. 7, 20 (left), and 71

Los Alamos National Library: p. 46

National Archives: pp. 1, 5, 6, 11, 14 (both), 15, 16 (bottom left), 17, 19, 20 (bottom right), 23, 29, 31, 32, 33, 34, 35, 38, 39, 40, 41, 42 (all), 43, 45, 47, 48, 49, 50 (top), 51, 54, 55, 56, 58, 59, 60, 61, 62, 63, 64, 65, 67, 70, 72, 73, 75, 79, 84 (inset), 86 (both), 87, 88, 89, 90, and 91

NYPL Office of Special Collections: p. 30

Popper Foto/Archive Photos: Front cover

Superstock, Inc.: p. 10

United Nations/Yuichiro Sasaki: p. 82

U.S. Air Force: pp. 16 (top right) and 44

U.S. Army: p. 50 (bottom)

U.S. Marine Corps: pp. 25

U.S. Navy: p. 18

TABLE OF CONTENTS

INTRODUCTION

World War II (1939–1945) was the greatest catastrophe in history. More than a half century after it ended, this conflict remains by far the most costly war of all time. More people were killed, more houses, apartment buildings, factories, bridges, and other works of man were destroyed than ever before or since.

The Axis Powers—Germany, Italy, and Japan—and their leaders—Adolf Hitler, Benito Mussolini, and General Hideki Tojo—posed the greatest threat Western civilization ever faced. At their height, the Axis had conquered or controlled almost all of Europe, North Africa from the Atlantic to Egypt, and vast sections of China and the Pacific. They came very close to winning the war, and if they had, they would have thrown the entire world into a second Dark Age. But instead of winning they were destroyed by the Allied powers led by the United States, Great Britain, the Soviet Union, and France. This was the number one outcome of the war.

For everyone, everywhere, World War II had a deep impact, continuing today to seize the imagination. The universal fascination with the war is all the greater because of its stakes, its scope, its high drama, its titanic battles, its larger-than-life leading actors, and its tragedies. But ultimately the fascination becomes specific, directed toward both the individual people—especially the American fighting men—who lived and died in the war and the places where they fought.

America sent her young men halfway around the world, in both directions, not to conquer, not to pillage, not to loot, not to rape, but to liberate. And they did, not only in the occupied countries but in Germany and Japan, too. One veteran, when asked what it all meant, said that he felt he had done his part in turning the twentieth century from one of darkness into one of light. Another said, "Listen, I was eighteen years old and had my whole life ahead of me. I had been taught the difference between right and wrong. And I didn't want to live in a world in which wrong prevailed. So I fought."

The day after D-Day, the Allied invasion of Normandy, France, against Hitler's Fortress Europe, Private Robert Healey and a friend returned to one of the landing sites, Omaha Beach, to retrieve their backpacks. They found battlefield debris everywhere, all kinds of equipment washing back and forth in the tide, and bodies of soldiers, many still lying where they had been killed. Pvt. Healey remembered one dead soldier, in particular. "I came across what was probably the most poignant memory I have of this whole episode. Lying on the beach was a young soldier, his arms outstretched. Near one of his hands, as if he had been reading it, was a pocketbook [paperback].

"It was *Our Hearts Were Young and Gay* by Cornelia Otis Skinner. This expressed the spirit of our ordeal. Our hearts were young and gay because we thought we were immortal, we believed we were doing a great thing, and we really believed in the crusade which we hoped would liberate the world from the heel of Nazism."

In the aftermath of World War II, slowly, surely, the spirit of those GIs handing out candy and helping to bring democracy to their former enemies spread, and today it is the democracies—not the totalitarians—who are on the march. Today, one can again believe in progress. This is in large part thanks to the GIs—along with the millions of others who helped liberate Germany and Japan from their fanatical rulers, then, later stood up to Russia's Josef Stalin and his successors. That generation has done more to spread freedom—and prosperity—around the globe than any previous generation.

What I think of the GIs more than a half century after their victory was best said by Sergeant Mike Ranney of the 101st: "In thinking back on the days of Easy Company, I'm treasuring my remark to a grandson who asked, 'Grandpa, were you a hero in the war?'

"'No,' I answered, 'but I served in a company of heroes.'"

So far as I am concerned, so did they all.

Above: Benito Mussolini and Adolf Hitler.

The seeds of World War II in Europe were planted in the harsh Treaty of Versailles, which ended World War I. In addition to blaming Germany for starting World War I, the treaty tried to stop Germany from becoming powerful enough to start another one.

Unfortunately the Treaty of Versailles made a lot of Germans angry. One man in particular, Adolf Hitler, leader of the National Socialist (Nazi) Party, used this nationwide resentment to bring himself to power. He promised to make Germany strong again, and he said that the only way Germany could regain its position as the greatest country in Europe was if it had more living space—*lebensraum*. Lots of Germans liked what he said and on January 30, 1933, he was appointed chancellor. Once in power he revealed how evil he was. He abolished unions, took away people's right to vote, and used his secret police, called the Gestapo, to put people who disagreed with him in jail or special prisons called concentration camps. Now Germany's *Führer* (leader), he started rearming the country and demanding that it get back what it had lost in World War I. On October 25, 1936, he formed the Rome-Berlin Axis with the Italian dictator Benito Mussolini. This alliance established a "new order in Europe" that would break the domination of Great Britain and France. On May 22, 1939 the alliance was made a formal treaty called the Pact of Steel.

At first the governments of Great Britain and France used the policy of appeasement with Germany, thinking that if they gave in to some of Hitler's demands, he would be satisfied and stop. They let Hitler take the country of Austria and make it a part of Germany (the *Anschluss*). They even signed a treaty, the Munich Agreement, that let Hitler take the part of Czechoslovakia that bordered Germany. But the more they let Hitler take, the more Hitler demanded. Finally the leaders of Great Britain and France saw that there was only one way to stop him: They would have to fight him. After Hitler ordered the invasion of Poland on September 1, 1939, the British and French governments declared war. World War II in Europe had begun.

Opposite: Adolf Hitler (center) at a Nazi Party rally in Nuremberg, Germany.

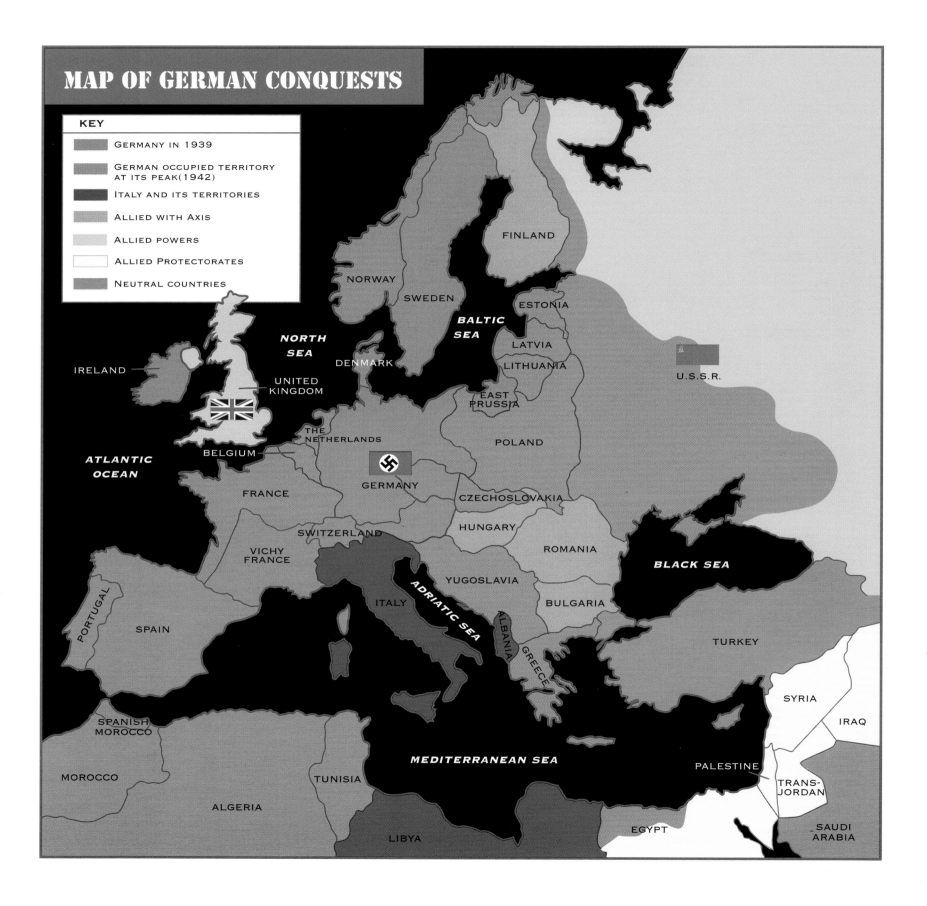

MAP OF GERMAN CONQUESTS

KEY
- Germany in 1939
- German occupied territory at its peak (1942)
- Italy and its territories
- Allied with Axis
- Allied powers
- Allied Protectorates
- Neutral countries

IRELAND

NORTH SEA

UNITED KINGDOM

ATLANTIC OCEAN

BELGIUM

THE NETHERLANDS

DENMARK

NORWAY

SWEDEN

FINLAND

BALTIC SEA

ESTONIA

LATVIA

LITHUANIA

EAST PRUSSIA

POLAND

U.S.S.R.

FRANCE

GERMANY

CZECHOSLOVAKIA

SWITZERLAND

VICHY FRANCE

HUNGARY

ROMANIA

BLACK SEA

ITALY

ADRIATIC SEA

YUGOSLAVIA

ALBANIA

GREECE

BULGARIA

TURKEY

PORTUGAL

SPAIN

SPANISH MOROCCO

MOROCCO

TUNISIA

MEDITERRANEAN SEA

ALGERIA

LIBYA

EGYPT

SYRIA

IRAQ

PALESTINE

TRANS-JORDAN

SAUDI ARABIA

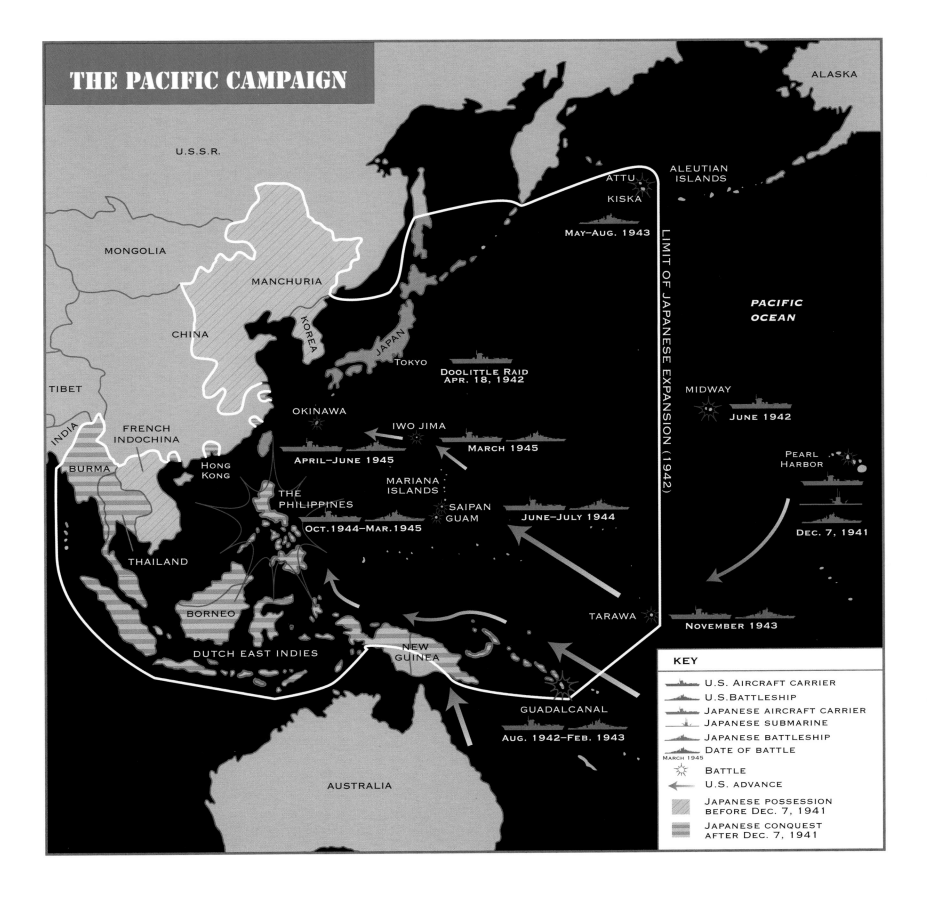

THE PACIFIC CAMPAIGN

ALASKA

U.S.S.R.

MONGOLIA

MANCHURIA

CHINA

KOREA

ALEUTIAN
ISLANDS

ATTU
KISKA

MAY–AUG. 1943

LIMIT OF JAPANESE EXPANSION (1942)

PACIFIC
OCEAN

JAPAN

TOKYO

Doolittle Raid
Apr. 18, 1942

MIDWAY

JUNE 1942

TIBET

OKINAWA

IWO JIMA

MARCH 1945

PEARL
HARBOR

INDIA

APRIL–JUNE 1945

MARIANA
ISLANDS

DEC. 7, 1941

FRENCH
INDOCHINA

Hong
Kong

THE
PHILIPPINES

SAIPAN
GUAM

JUNE–JULY 1944

BURMA

Oct.1944–Mar.1945

THAILAND

BORNEO

TARAWA

NOVEMBER 1943

DUTCH EAST INDIES

NEW
GUINEA

GUADALCANAL

AUG. 1942–FEB. 1943

AUSTRALIA

KEY

U.S. AIRCRAFT CARRIER

U.S. BATTLESHIP

JAPANESE AIRCRAFT CARRIER

JAPANESE SUBMARINE

JAPANESE BATTLESHIP

DATE OF BATTLE

MARCH 1945

BATTLE

U.S. ADVANCE

JAPANESE POSSESSION
BEFORE DEC. 7, 1941

JAPANESE CONQUEST
AFTER DEC. 7, 1941

As Hitler was gaining power as leader of Germany, in Asia, Japan was growing increasingly powerful, both economically and militarily. But Japan had two big problems: It had very little land and a lot of people. The only way it could keep growing was to import food and raw materials to feed its people and supply its industry. Also, it was not treated as an equal by the other big industrial countries. This angered Japan because it had been an ally of Great Britain, France, the United States, and Italy during World War I.

Between World War I and World War II the Japanese Army and Navy grew more powerful and aggressive. Eventually they seized control of the government. General Hideki Tojo was the Japanese Minister of War and one of the military leaders who believed that the only way Japan would be treated equally was if it took what it wanted and needed by force. In 1937, instead of signing a trade agreement with China, Japan chose to attack and keep the parts of China it had invaded.

America demanded that Japan halt its invasion of China and return the land it had conquered. Japan refused. So the United States stopped all shipments of raw materials that Japan needed, including oil, iron ore, and other metals, issuing a trade embargo against them.

On October 17, 1941, Tojo, who had become the Prime Minister of Japan, told Emperor Hirohito that if Japan did not immediately take strong action against the United States, he feared Japan would become a third-class nation in two or three years.

On November 5, 1941, with the emperor's agreement, the Japanese government secretly made the decision to go to war. On December 7, 1941, Japanese carrier-borne airplanes launched a surprise attack on the U.S. military bases and port at Pearl Harbor, Hawaii. World War II in the Pacific had begun.

Above: Hirohito, Emperor of Japan.

Opposite: A child cries after a Japanese bombing raid of Shanghai, China.

QUICK FACTS

⭐ The Japanese Navy launched 2 air strikes against Pearl Harbor and the nearby military airfields on Oahu. The first wave had 183 planes containing 40 torpedo bombers, 51 dive-bombers, 49 bombers, and 43 fighters. The second wave had 170 planes containing 80 dive-bombers, 54 bombers, and 36 fighters.

⭐ There were 96 ships anchored in Pearl Harbor. 18 ships were sunk or seriously damaged, including 8 battleships, and over 4,600 men were killed or wounded.

⭐ The Japanese lost 29 aircraft, 1 submarine, and 5 two-man midget submarines.

⭐ In 1941 Hawaii was a U.S. territory. It didn't become the 50th state until 1959.

Above: Admiral Isoroku Yamamoto, planner of the attack on Pearl Harbor.

It was becoming obvious to people who knew the facts that war between Japan and the United States was inevitable. President Roosevelt ordered his military commanders in the Pacific to go on the alert, especially General Douglas MacArthur in the Philippines, and Admiral Husband Kimmel and General Walter Short, who were responsible for U.S. forces in and around the big Navy base at Pearl Harbor, Hawaii. Adm. Kimmel and Gen. Short believed that the biggest threats they faced were sabotage and submarine attack. They thought that the military bases in and around Pearl Harbor were too strong and well protected to be attacked openly.

Then, at 7:53 A.M. on Sunday, December 7, 1941, Lieutenant Commander Mitsuo Fuchida, in his lead Japanese bomber, called out on his radio, "Tora! Tora! Tora!" (Tiger! Tiger! Tiger!). It was the code-word that signaled that the Imperial Japanese Navy had achieved maximum strategic surprise over U.S. Army and Navy forces based in and around Pearl Harbor. At 7:55 A.M., the Japanese war planes attacked.

By the time the attack had ended, the Imperial Japanese Navy had accomplished its goal of crippling the U.S. Pacific Fleet. Most of the fleet was at the bottom of the harbor, and most of the Army, Navy, and Marine fighter planes and bombers were smoking ruins.

Forty-six minutes after the first bombs and torpedoes had been dropped, the Japanese ambassadors delivered their country's declaration of war on the United States to U.S. Secretary of State Cordell Hull. Hull had already heard of the attack on Pearl Harbor, and he was outraged at Japan's treachery.

It was "a date which will live in infamy," said President Franklin D. Roosevelt on December 8th when he asked Congress to declare war on Japan.

"Remember Pearl Harbor!" became the war cry across the nation as young men enlisted in the Army, Navy, Army Air Force, and Marines by the hundreds of thousands.

When Japan's Axis allies, Hitler and Mussolini, honored their treaty obligation and declared war on the United States four days later, the conflict had truly become a world war.

Opposite: U.S. Navy battleships sunk by Japanese warplanes.

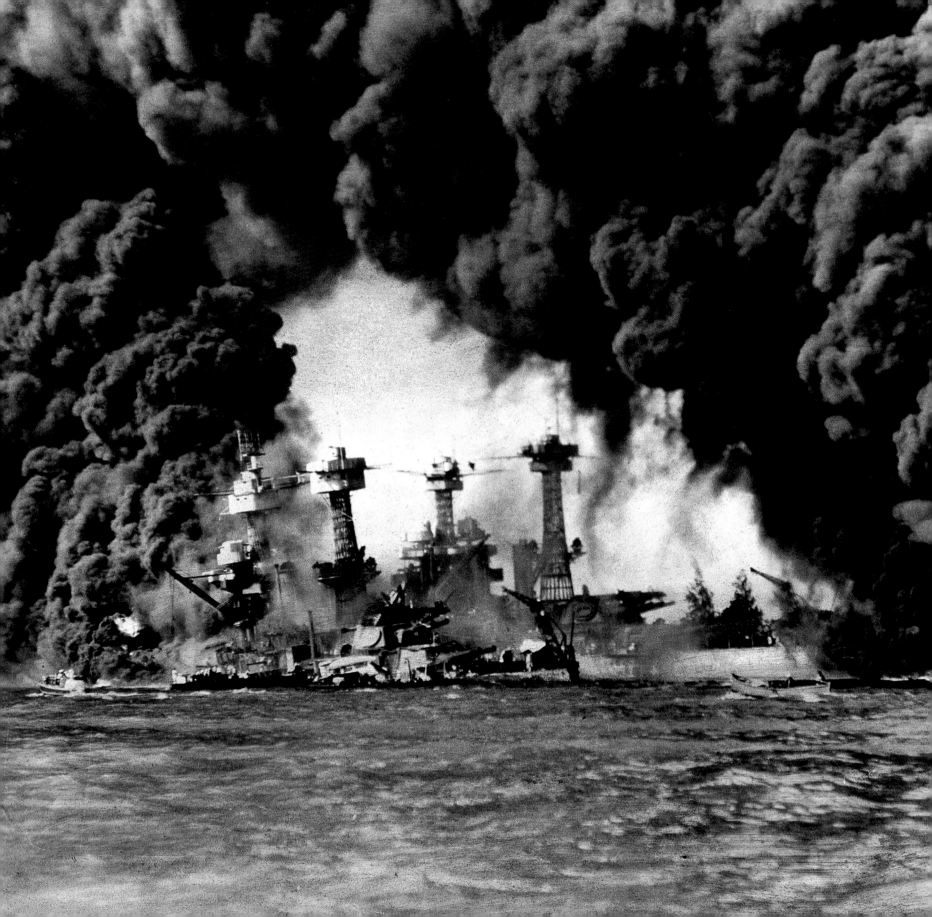

QUICK FACTS

★ Officers were needed so fast that lieutenants were trained in three months and were called Ninety-Day Wonders.

★ General George C. Marshall was the leader of the U.S. Army and Army Air Force.

★ Admiral Ernest J. King was the leader of the Navy.

★ The Air Force was a part of the Army in World War II. It did not become a separate branch of the military until after the war.

★ In 1941 a private earned $21 a month.

★ In 1942 a private earned $50 a month.

Man the GUNS
Join the NAVY

The United States was unprepared for war. Many people and politicians were "isolationists" who saw no reason why their country should fight Germany or Japan.

All that changed with the attack on Pearl Harbor. In 1939 the U.S. Army had 190,000 men. By 1945 it would have 10.4 million! Millions more were in the Navy, Marines, and Army Air Force. Newly enlisted men would march onto bases that were still under construction. Car companies stopped making cars for civilians and started making jeeps, trucks, tanks, and other vehicles for the military. Tire companies had to create synthetic rubber because Japan had captured the only countries in the world that produced natural rubber.

Men trained using wooden rifles, flour bags for grenades, and trucks as tanks. Young men who had been mechanics, soda jerks, and farmhands were now learning how to march, shoot, build bridges under fire, or cook dozens of meals out in the open and in the rain.

Seventeen-year-old boys lied about their age so they could enlist. One young man was Private Ken Russell who would become a paratrooper participating in the D-Day invasion of Normandy, France. On the night of June 5, 1944, while flying over the English Channel on his way to Normandy, he was struck by the thought that his high school class back in Tennessee was graduating that night.

Hitler thought that Americans were soft and would make poor soldiers. But the Americans were determined to quickly learn the unfamiliar trade of war and use that knowledge to defeat Germany and Japan.

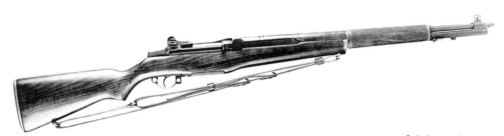

Left: A recruitment poster.
Above: An M1 Garand rifle.
Opposite: Black soldiers training. Note the obsolete World War I-era helmets.

QUICK FACTS

⭐ Because they were too big to land on carrier decks after bombing Japan, the B-25s flew to Allied airfields in China.

⭐ Lt. Col. Doolittle was awarded the Medal of Honor for the raid.

⭐ When asked where the bombers had come from, President Roosevelt said, "Shangri-La." Shangri-La was a mythical land in a popular movie of the day.

⭐ The Doolittle Raid caused the Japanese high command to attack Midway.

⭐ The Army Air Corps was renamed the Army Air Force in June 1941.

Above: Adm. William Halsey.
Upper right: Lt. Col. James H. Doolittle.
Opposite: Lt. Col. Doolittle's B-25 takes off from the flight deck of the USS *Hornet.*

After Japan's attack on Pearl Harbor, President Roosevelt knew America somehow had to quickly strike back against Japan to boost the morale of the American people who were growing increasingly upset as they heard and read about one Japanese victory after another in the Pacific.

Army Air Force Lieutenant Colonel James H. "Jimmy" Doolittle had a radical plan. He proposed that the United States launch an air raid on Japan using Army Air Force B-25 Mitchell bombers that would take off from Navy aircraft carriers. At first his superiors thought he was crazy. They thought it was impossible for a big, heavy bomber like the B-25 to take off from the short flight deck of an aircraft carrier. Doolittle demonstrated that it was possible, and he convinced the skeptics to approve his plan.

On April 18, 1942, at 8:20 A.M. Lt. Col. Doolittle flew his B-25 off the deck of the USS *Hornet.* Eyewitnesses said it was scary watching the sixteen bombers in the mission taxi down the oh-so-small flight deck. "When Jimmy's plane buzzed down the *Hornet's* deck, there wasn't a man who didn't help sweat him into the air," said Admiral William "Bull" Halsey, the Navy commander of the operation.

The bombing raid did little physical damage to Japan. But the psychological impact was huge. The Japanese civilians were panic-stricken. The Imperial Army and Navy had promised that their homeland would never be attacked. But it was, sooner than the military leaders thought possible—and by a completely unexpected weapon, Army Air Force land-based bombers! For the first time the Japanese leaders who had rushed to war saw that they were dealing with an enemy more dangerous than they had imagined.

QUICK FACTS

★ The Japanese armada totaled 190 ships, including 8 aircraft carriers, and 11 battleships. The U.S. fleet totaled fewer than 40 ships, contained 3 aircraft carriers (1 crippled) and no battleships.

★ *Enterprise* cooks baked 10,000 ginger spice cookies for the crew on the day of the battle.

★ Movie director John Ford was on Midway Island and shot a documentary of the battle for the U.S. government.

★ Commander Joseph J. Rochefort Jr. cracked the Japanese naval code that told of the invasion plans.

★ Midway is an atoll, a ring of coral islands in the ocean. Its largest islands are Eastern and Sand Islands. The total land area on Midway is 3 square miles.

It was the spring of 1942. Japanese forces had defeated the British in Hong Kong, Burma, Malaya, and Singapore. They had captured the Netherlands East Indies and the American possessions of the Philippines, Guam, and Wake Island. The Imperial Japanese Navy bloodied the U.S. Navy in the Battle of Coral Sea, sinking the aircraft carrier *Lexington* and badly damaging a second, *Yorktown*. To complete the outer ring of defense around Japan, and prevent another Doolittle Raid on Japan, Admiral Yamamoto wanted to seize the strategic outpost island of Midway. With Midway and its valuable airfields in his possession, nothing could sail the sea north and west of Hawaii without his knowledge.

Commander-in-Chief Pacific Fleet (CinCPAC) Admiral Chester W. Nimitz knew this too. That's why he had to stop the Japanese. Two aircraft carriers, *Enterprise* and *Hornet,* and their support ships were on their way to defend Midway. Nimitz had been told that *Yorktown*'s repairs would take at least ninety days. When it arrived at Pearl Harbor he told the repair crew, "We must have this ship back in three days."

Marine pilot Major Lofton Henderson, based on Midway, knew that the enemy's planes were modern and deadly and that America's dive-bombers, torpedo planes, and fighters were obsolete and slow. On the day of battle Maj. Henderson told the men in his squadron of dive-bombers that because of this, the mission to attack the Japanese fleet would be voluntary. His men all followed him.

At the same time, pilots on the carriers *Enterprise, Hornet,* and *Yorktown,* which *was* repaired in three days, took off to the attack. It was a battle that the outnumbered and outclassed Americans had no right to win. But at the end of the day of June 4, 1942, four mighty Japanese carriers were destroyed. The invasion was forced to retreat. The aura of Japanese invincibility, cracked during the Doolittle Raid, was shattered at Midway.

Above: Japanese heavy cruiser *Mikuma.*

Opposite: U.S. Navy Dauntless dive-bombers preparing to attack the Japanese fleet.

QUICK FACTS

⭐ 37% of the population of Hawaii was of Japanese descent.

⭐ There was never any evidence of espionage or sabotage by Japanese-Americans.

⭐ The 100th Battalion was called the Purple Heart Battalion because it had so many combat casualties.

⭐ There were 10 relocation centers. The last was closed in 1946.

They were immigrants who believed in the American way as strongly as their fellow Polish, German, Irish, Italian, and other European immigrants. But in the aftermath of Pearl Harbor, war hysteria caused Japanese-Americans to be singled out for unprecedented discrimination—all were suspect.

President Roosevelt signed Executive Order 9066, authorizing the relocation of Japanese-Americans to "military areas." More than 110,000 people in California alone had their homes and businesses confiscated and were forced to move to isolated relocation camps.

This was unfair and unjustified treatment. But what so many people didn't realize was that the *Nisei*—the Japanese word for "second," meaning second generation—were native-born American citizens, too, and they hated what Japan had done to their country. When recruiters visited the camps, young Nisei men volunteered for the military. Fifteen hundred Nisei members of the Hawaiian National Guard were formed into the U.S. Army's 100th Battalion. Ten thousand Nisei volunteered for the Nisei regiment, the 442nd. In addition, Nisei were invaluable interpreters and translators in the Pacific war.

Fighting in Italy and France, the 442nd became the most highly decorated regiment in the Army, and the 100th Battalion won three Distinguished Unit Citations, an extraordinary achievement.

Forty years later, Congress apologized and authorized a payment of $20,000 to each internee. In ceremonies at the White House on June 22, 2000, twenty-one Nisei WWII veterans were awarded our nation's highest decoration for valor, the Medal of Honor.

Above: Sign on an Oakland, California, store owned by a Japanese-American.
Right: A Japanese-American World War I veteran.
Opposite: A Japanese-American girl being processed for internment.

QUICK FACTS

★ The German Navy had only 56 U-boats at the start of the war. By the end of the war in 1945 they had built 1,170.

★ German U-boats sank 2,000 Allied ships at a cost of 781 U-boats destroyed.

★ In September and October of 1941, before the U.S. was officially at war with Germany, U-boats attacked and damaged the U.S. destroyers *Greer* and *Kearney* and on October 31 the destroyer *Reuben James*.

★ The United States used prefabricated designs for the merchant (supply) ships. The average construction time was three months.

★ The 10,000-ton Liberty-class merchant ship *Robert E. Peary* was constructed in 4 days and 15 hours.

In Europe, Hitler followed up his conquest of Poland with an attack on the Netherlands, Belgium, Luxembourg, and France. His German Army defeated them all. Then on June 22, 1941, he attacked the Soviet Union. By December his armies had reached the suburbs of Moscow, almost 1,000 miles away from Berlin, the capital of Germany. Great Britain, separated from the continent by the English Channel, was the only European country that remained undefeated and unoccupied. But Great Britain could still be beaten. Hitler knew that if he could stop merchant ships from delivering supplies to Great Britain, he could force it to surrender. He ordered his Navy, and particularly his deadly submarines, called U-boats, to search the Atlantic Ocean for merchant ships heading for England and sink them.

The German surface Navy had some early success, but the U-boats were Hitler's mightiest weapon in the Battle of the Atlantic. At first alone, then in deadly "Wolf Packs," the U-boats became the scourge of the Atlantic, sinking ships as close as inside the English ports and as far away as South Africa, Brazil, the Caribbean, the Gulf Coast, and all along the East Coast of the United States.

Working together, the Americans and the British created weapons and plans to defeat the U-boats. They created a convoy system that grouped supply ships together so warships could better protect them. They developed sonar, which used sound waves to help warships "see" U-boats underwater. Special sub-chasing airplanes were built, too. And American shipbuilders were able to make supply ships faster than the U-boats could sink them.

British Prime Minister Winston Churchill later said, "The only thing that ever frightened me during the war was the U-boat peril. It was our worst evil."

Left: A German U-boat captain.
Opposite: A merchant ship victim of a U-boat attack.

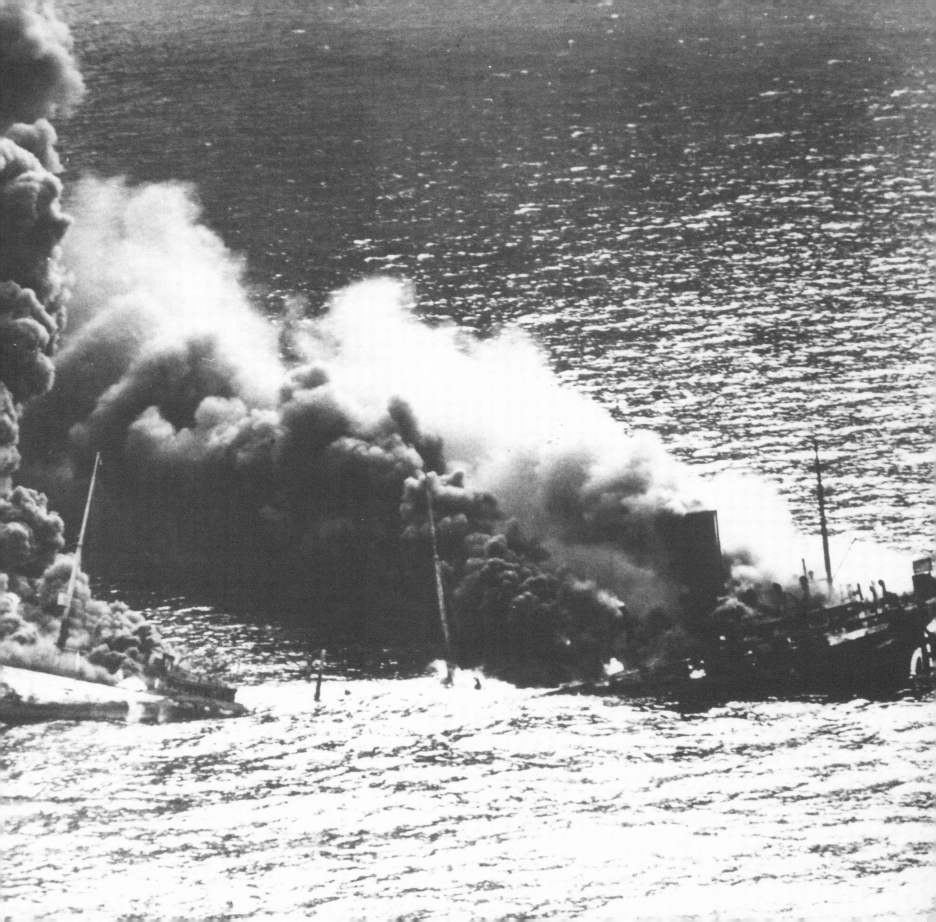

QUICK FACTS

⭐ Military planners gave each operation a code name. The code name for the invasion of Guadalcanal was Cactus.

⭐ Guadalcanal is 90 miles long and 25 miles wide and is at the eastern end of the Solomon Islands chain.

⭐ Seven major naval battles were fought over Guadalcanal.

⭐ So many ships were sunk in the channel north of Guadalcanal that it got the nickname Ironbottom Sound.

⭐ The captured airfield was named Henderson Field after Marine pilot Major Lofton Henderson who was killed attacking the Japanese carriers at Midway.

Below: A Wildcat fighter plane taking off from Henderson Field.
Opposite: Guadalcanal after a tropical storm.

After the Battle of Midway, a stalemate situation existed between Japan and the United States. Japanese forces were constructing an airfield on Guadalcanal, one of the Solomon Islands, only 1,200 miles from Australia. Once the airfield was finished, Japanese warplanes could easily attack Australia. American strategists could not let that happen, so Guadalcanal became the place where the United States committed its men and ships to its first full offensive.

On August 7, 1942, 19,000 men of the 1st Marine Division invaded, supported by Navy warships and supply ships. Though the landing went smoothly, everything after that seemed to go wrong. The Japanese Navy swiftly counterattacked at night and forced the U.S. Navy to retreat with their supply transports only half unloaded.

Isolated, short of food and ammunition, weakened by tropical diseases, the Marines desperately fought against the Japanese. People in the United States were worried that the Japanese would win. Even Marine Major General Alexander Vandegrift, who commanded the invasion force, later said there were "a hundred reasons why this operation should fail."

But it did not fail. At times fighting barefoot because there were no replacements for their rotted boots, the Marines beat back attack after attack. Ultimately reinforced and resupplied, the Marines finally defeated the Japanese and took Guadalcanal.

The Japanese still held most of the islands in the Pacific. Now America's senior commanders had to decide whether to invade each individual island and slowly, step by step, advance toward Japan, or to pick and choose the most important islands and leapfrog over the others. The leapfrog method was chosen because America's leaders believed it would cost fewer lives and would shorten the war. This strategy became known as the island-hopping campaign.

THE BATTLE OF GUADALCANAL

SAVO
ISLAND

FLORIDA
ISLAND

PACIFIC OCEAN

OPERATION CACTUS
AUGUST 7, 1942

IRONBOTTOM SOUND

FEBRUARY 1943

OCTOBER 1942

AUGUST 1942

SEPTEMBER 1942

GUADALCANAL

CORAL SEA

KEY

 JAPANESE PATH OF ATTACK

 U.S. MARINE PATH OF ATTACK

 INVASION SITE

 U.S. MARINE PERIMETER

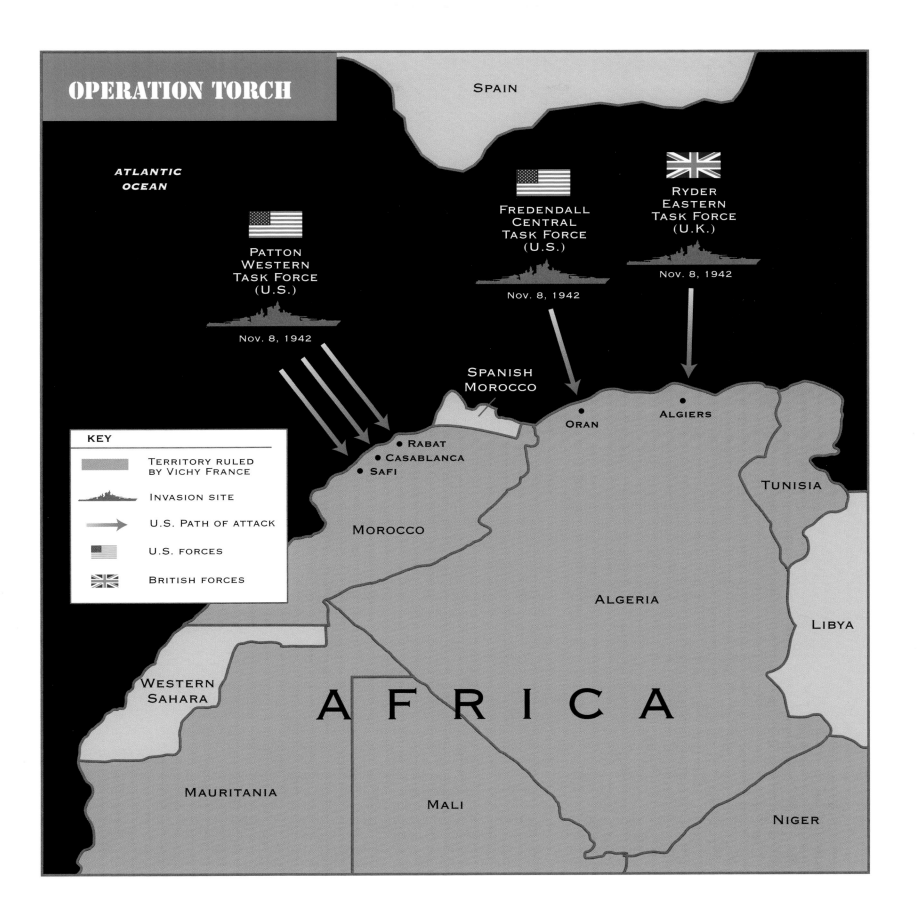

QUICK FACTS

⭐ When Germany defeated France in 1940, the French government moved from Paris to the city of Vichy. The Allies called the people, military and civilian, who worked for this pro-Nazi government "Vichy French." Their leader was Premier Henri Pétain.

⭐ Lieutenant General Dwight D. Eisenhower was the commander-in-chief of the Allied invasion forces.

⭐ Three separate task forces made up the invasion, two American, one British.

⭐ General Robert Eichelberger was the original commander of the Western Task Force. Transferred to the Pacific, he was replaced by Maj. Gen. Patton.

Above: Lt. Gen. Dwight D. Eisenhower.
Opposite: German prisoners of war (POWs) getting food supplies.

In 1942, from the northern shores of Norway high above the Arctic Circle to the deserts of Egypt, from the Atlantic Coast of France to the eastern shore of the Black Sea in Russia, the German Army *blitzkrieg* (lightning war) had shattered some of the greatest armies in the world. Josef Stalin, the leader of the Soviet Union, demanded the United States and Great Britain quickly invade Europe, opening a "second front" to pull German troops away from his desperately fighting armies on the Russian front.

Struggling to train the new soldiers and sailors, manufacture war supplies, and meet its commitments in the Pacific, America in 1942 was still too weak to launch a direct attack on Europe itself. So Allied leaders chose to invade French North Africa because the Axis defenses were not as strong there as they were in Nazi-controlled Europe. Here, it was judged, the green American troops would have the best chance of success. On November 8, 1942, Operation Torch was launched.

At first, the inexperienced American soldiers suffered much chaos on the beaches. But they adapted quickly, capturing their objectives. Typical was the initiative and courage displayed by Second Lieutenant S. W. Sprindis, a platoon leader who with only forty men held a strategic lighthouse against attacks by a Vichy French battalion of 1,000 men. After the battle Western Task Force Commander Major General George Patton visited Sprindis, asking him, "Lieutenant, what is your rank?"

"Second Lieutenant, sir," replied Sprindis.

"You are a liar, sir, you are now a First Lieutenant," said Patton, rewarding him an on-the-spot promotion.

Corporal Morris Zimmerman reflected the attitude of many of the new soldiers who suddenly found themselves in faraway lands. Writing to his mother, he said, "This is your son reporting from the land of Arabs and wine, sticky flies and red sand. I have always wanted to cross an ocean to see what was on the other side and darned if I didn't." He closed his letter with words of reassurance used by soldiers and sailors in all the campaign theaters, "I am all right and will try and take care of myself."

QUICK FACTS

⭐ The Aleutian Islands chain is 1,200 miles long and contains over 100 islands.

⭐ Dutch Harbor, the primary military base for the campaign, is 1,000 miles from Attu and Kiska.

⭐ The Alcan (Alaska-Canada) Highway was built to supply war materials to Alaska and the Soviet Union. It was constructed almost entirely by black troops.

⭐ It got so cold in the winter that engine oil would freeze as hard as a rock.

⭐ Mount Ballyhoo, near Dutch Harbor, was christened by writer Jack London, who visited Dutch Harbor and used it as a setting in his novel *The Sea Wolf.*

When the Japanese attacked Midway, a part of it also invaded Attu and Kiska, the westernmost islands in Alaska's Aleutian Islands chain.

It took fourteen months for Allied forces to liberate the islands. The battle was fought in the worst weather imaginable and under the most primitive of conditions. Thick, dense fog was a constant danger. Gale-force winds called williwaws blew down buildings, flipped over parked airplanes, and ripped up the metal surface of the runways. Often pilots would have to fly as low as twenty-five feet above the ocean just to be able to see. Temperatures in the summertime were just above freezing, but dampness and windchill would drop the temperature to just above zero degrees Fahrenheit.

Major Jack Chennault, commander of the 11th Fighter Squadron, said, "We fueled our own planes from drums, slept in rude huts and bedrolls, and froze all the time."

Sergeant George R. McBride wrote, "I had to walk about a mile across the open tundra to get to my weather station. . . . With that wind, a parka was little better than a T-shirt. In the station, with oil stoves going, there was a 100-degree difference in temperature between floor and ceiling." At the air base on the Alaskan island of Kodiak, pilots would often have to circle the field before landing while ground crews chased bears off the runway.

On May 11, 1943, American soldiers liberated the westernmost island of Attu despite heavy losses. Next, Major General Simon Bolivar Buckner Jr., commander of the Allied troops in Alaska, prepared to free Kiska. On August 15, 1943, a combined U.S. and Canadian force landed unopposed. It would take days of cautious and thorough searching of the island before they discovered the amazing truth—the Japanese garrison had secretly evacuated more than two weeks earlier!

Left: On Adak, in the Aleutian Islands, African-American and white troops gather in a rare integrated event, a luncheon with President Roosevelt (in circle). *Opposite:* American troops land on Kiska Island.

QUICK FACTS

⭐ In the invasion, 180,000 troops and 2,590 ships were used, second only to D-Day.

⭐ The land area of Sicily is 10,000 square miles.

⭐ Mt. Etna on the northeast coast is 11,872 feet high.

⭐ Lt. Gen. Patton was almost sent home in disgrace for slapping two enlisted men who were suffering from battle fatigue.

⭐ War correspondent Ernie Pyle gave Major General Omar Bradley the nickname "the GI General" in Sicily.

All of North Africa had been liberated. President Roosevelt, Prime Minister Winston Churchill, and their advisers met in Casablanca to decide the next major target. It would be the Italian island of Sicily. Conquering Sicily would further chase the Axis out of the Mediterranean Sea and, the Allied leaders hoped, cause Italy to think about surrendering. On July 10, 1943, the British Eighth Army, under General Bernard Montgomery, and the U.S. Seventh Army, under Lieutenant General George Patton, invaded.

Landing near Gela, a town on the south-central coast of Sicily, the Americans encountered tough resistance. To help protect the landing, a Ranger force led by Lieutenant Colonel William Darby launched a diversionary attack on the town itself. They not only succeeded in clearing the entire town of enemy troops, they also repelled a vicious counterattack. Gen. Patton was so impressed by Darby, who won the Distinguished Service Cross in the battle, that he offered him a promotion to full colonel and his own regiment. Darby refused, saying that he wanted to stay with the men he loved, his Rangers. It was the first time in Patton's experience that anyone had ever turned down a promotion. He left amazed, thinking, Darby is a really great soldier.

The terrain in Sicily was so rugged, the only way to get supplies to the soldiers was by pack animal. Major General Lucian Truscott rounded up North African burros for this purpose. When he asked the Navy to transport them, they refused. Livestock—on *warships?* Never! Truscott explained that where he was going a burro was really "a weapon." Was the Navy going to refuse to ship Truscott's division's weapons to Sicily? Suddenly that changed everything—if these smelly, ship-fouling creatures weren't livestock, but *weapons*, then of course the Navy could help.

Left: Soldiers getting a shipload of burros ready for work in Sicily's mountainous trails.
Opposite: An Army corpsman tends to a wounded soldier.

Above: Italian children celebrating the liberation of Rome.
Opposite: Black troops clearing mines on a beach in Italy.

After the Allies had captured Sicily, most Italians wanted to end the war. Mussolini tried to bully his chief subordinates into sticking with Hitler. But they forced him to resign on July 26, 1943. The new Italian leader, Marshal Pietro Badoglio, opened secret surrender talks with the Allies. Italy signed the surrender treaty on September 3, 1943. But Hitler found out. Before the Allies could take advantage of the surrender, German armies swiftly seized control of the country.

Though Italy was called the "soft underbelly of Europe" by Churchill, the bloody battles of Cassino and Anzio, the cold and the rain, the mountains and ravines and countless river valleys proved that the Italian Campaign was anything but "soft." Still, Rome was liberated on June 5, 1944, a day before the D-Day invasion. By the time the war ended, Allied armies had reached the Austrian border.

One of the many divisions that distinguished itself in Italy was the African-American 92nd Division. Throughout its many branches, the Army segregated its black troopers and, for the most part, would not allow them into combat. It was ironic that the world's greatest democracy fought the world's greatest racist with a segregated Army. But in the winter of 1944–45, General Eisenhower asked for Negro volunteers for frontline units and 4,562 left their jobs of searching for mines, unloading ships, or driving trucks in order to fight. Black sergeants had to give up their stripes in order to become privates in an integrated unit. Many performed well, even magnificently. One battalion commander in the 78th Division said of his experience, "White men and colored men are welded together with a deep friendship and respect born of combat and matured by a realization that such an association is not the impossibility that many of us have been led to believe. When men undergo the same privations, face the same dangers, there can be no segregation." The black soldiers' conduct was so impressive that the Army brass changed its mind about black troopers and began the process of integrating them into white units. Within a decade the Army had emerged from being one of the most strictly segregated organizations in the country to the most successfully integrated.

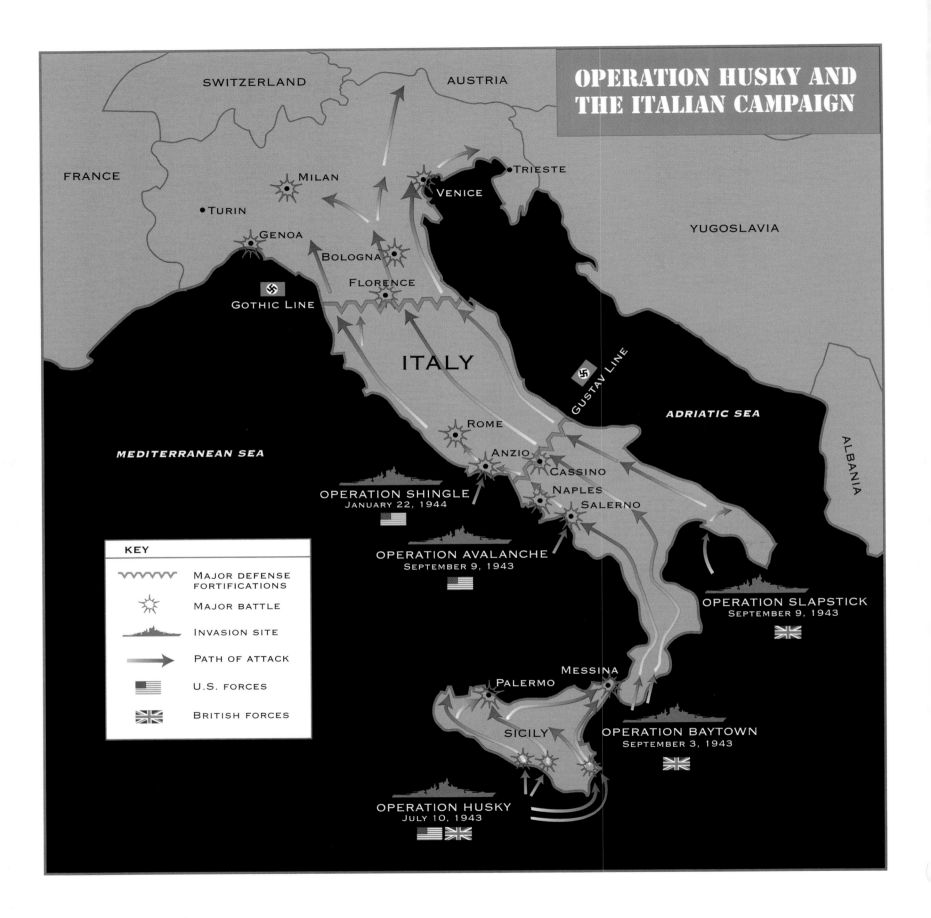

OPERATION HUSKY AND THE ITALIAN CAMPAIGN

SWITZERLAND

AUSTRIA

FRANCE

MILAN

TURIN

GENOA

BOLOGNA

FLORENCE

GOTHIC LINE

ITALY

TRIESTE

VENICE

YUGOSLAVIA

GUSTAV LINE

ADRIATIC SEA

ALBANIA

MEDITERRANEAN SEA

ROME

ANZIO

CASSINO

NAPLES

SALERNO

OPERATION SHINGLE
JANUARY 22, 1944

OPERATION AVALANCHE
SEPTEMBER 9, 1943

OPERATION SLAPSTICK
SEPTEMBER 9, 1943

KEY

〰️	MAJOR DEFENSE FORTIFICATIONS
✳️	MAJOR BATTLE
🚢	INVASION SITE
➡️	PATH OF ATTACK
🇺🇸	U.S. FORCES
🇬🇧	BRITISH FORCES

MESSINA

PALERMO

SICILY

OPERATION BAYTOWN
SEPTEMBER 3, 1943

OPERATION HUSKY
JULY 10, 1943

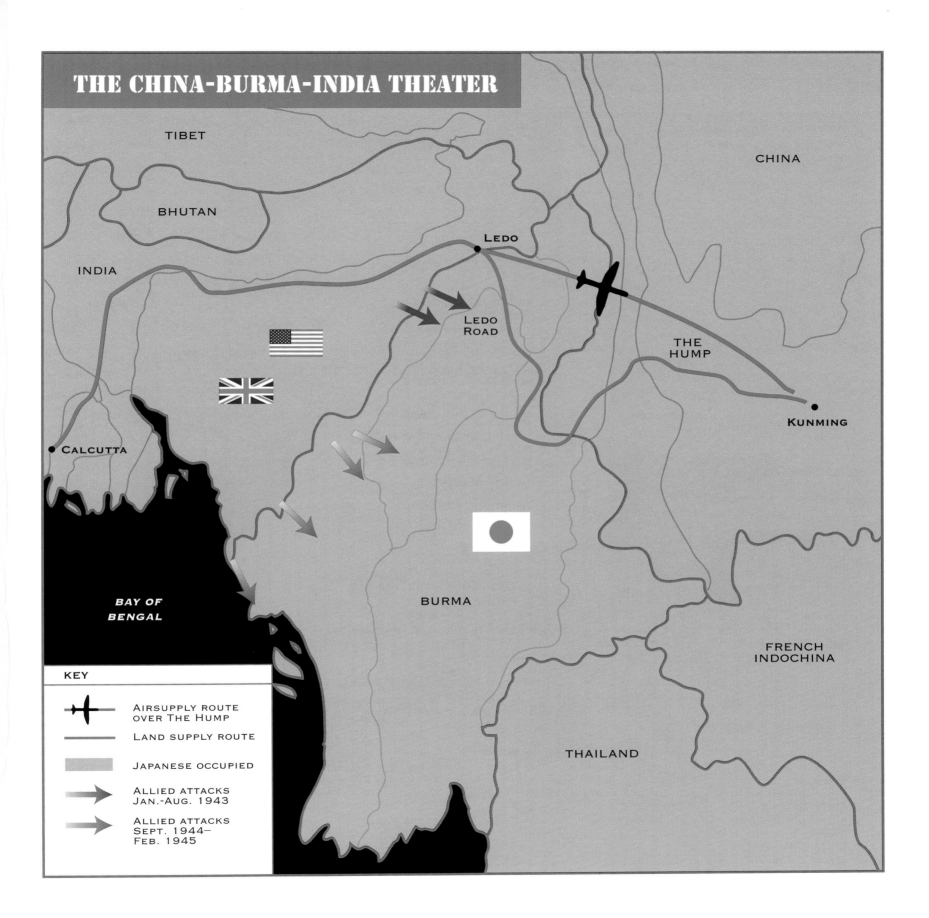

THE CHINA-BURMA-INDIA THEATER

TIBET

CHINA

BHUTAN

LEDO

INDIA

LEDO
ROAD

THE
HUMP

KUNMING

CALCUTTA

BAY OF
BENGAL

BURMA

FRENCH
INDOCHINA

THAILAND

KEY

Airsupply route
over The Hump

Land supply route

Japanese occupied

Allied attacks
Jan.-Aug. 1943

Allied attacks
Sept. 1944–
Feb. 1945

QUICK FACTS

⭐ The Ledo Road was 478 miles long, took 2 years and 23 days to build and was constructed mostly by African-American troops and Chinese coolies.

⭐ The CBI Theater of Operations came to be known as the Forgotten War because it received the least amount of men, supplies, and publicity compared with the other places where the war was fought.

⭐ The creation of Merrill's Marauders was inspired by British Major General Orde Wingate's guerilla fighters known officially as the Special Long-Range Penetration Group, who were nicknamed the Chindits after the Chinthe, a Burmese mythical creature that was half lion and half eagle.

⭐ The tallest peak along the Hump route was the 22,000-foot Tali.

⭐ From 1942–1945, 650,000 tons of supplies were carried over the Hump to China.

The China-Burma-India Theater of Operations, or CBI, as it was commonly known, was on the opposite side of the world. On one side it had the Himalayas, on the other it had the tropical jungles of Burma. In order of priorities for men and equipment, it came in at a distant third after Europe and the Pacific. Yet somehow Lieutenant General Joseph "Vinegar Joe" Stilwell had to maintain the strategic goals given him: Prevent Japan from invading India, and supply the Nationalist Chinese forces led by Chiang Kai-shek in their ongoing fight against Japan.

When Japan conquered Burma and closed off the overland supply route to China, the Air Transport Command was created to fly in supplies over the Hump, as the Himalayas were called. At the same time, construction was begun on a new overland route in northeast India called the Ledo Road.

The forces in the CBI theater of operations ranged from the dashing and romantic volunteer aviators of the Flying Tigers, who flew P-40 Warhawks painted with sharks' mouths, to guerilla fighters, including the 5307th Provisional Unit, Merrill's Marauders, which proved to be as good at jungle fighting as the Japanese.

Despite fighting on a shoestring, the forces in the CBI managed to liberate Burma and keep enough supplies going to China to keep it in the war.

Right: Chiang Kai-shek, Madam Chiang, and Lt. Gen. Joseph Stilwell.
Opposite: P-40 fighter planes from the Flying Tigers and a B-24 Liberator bomber.

QUICK FACTS

⭐ Betio is the main island in the Tarawa atoll. It is about the size of New York City's Central Park.

⭐ Tarawa is a part of the Gilbert Islands archipelago. It is 2,500 miles southwest of Hawaii.

⭐ Tarawa is surrounded by treacherous and unpredictable tides. These delayed the landings of the Marines.

⭐ New amphibious Landing Vehicle Tanks (LVTs) were used by the Americans for the first time. They worked well, but there were not enough for the battle.

⭐ More than 1,000 Marines and seamen fell at Tarawa, and another 2,100 were wounded. The Japanese lost over 5,000 men.

Operation Galvanic, the invasion of the Tarawa and Makin atolls, was the first step in the island-hopping campaign designed to sweep across the Central Pacific and cut off Japan from its resource-rich conquests in the south.

Eighteen thousand Marines landed on Tarawa on November 20, 1943. They were using new amphibious landing equipment and new invasion techniques for the first time. What they did not know was that the defenses on Tarawa were an interlocking series of fortifications of underground bunkers and above-ground pillboxes (so called because they looked like the containers used to hold prescription drugs). Both the bunkers and the pillboxes were structures built of steel and concrete so thick and strong that even a direct hit from a bomb or a cannon shell could not destroy them. They were then covered with sand and trees so that it was almost impossible to spot them. The Japanese commander of Tarawa had boasted that the Americans could not take Tarawa with a million men in a hundred years.

At first it seemed the commander would make good on his boast. Most of the landing craft got stranded on a reef in front of the invasion beach. The Marines who got onshore discovered a maze of camouflaged underground bunkers and pillboxes that had not been touched by the preinvasion bombardment. The Japanese soldiers inside the defenses used their machine guns and small cannons with deadly efficiency. By sundown of the first day the situation for the Americans looked grim.

But the individual courage and initiative of the Marines tipped the balance. Tarawa was captured within a week, but the terrible cost of the battle was a sobering lesson for everyone in the United States. Defeat of Japan and the end of the war seemed very far away indeed.

Left: Marines assaulting a Japanese strongpoint.
Opposite: Marines wading through the lagoon.

QUICK FACTS

⭐ American factories produced 300,000 military aircraft, 89,000 tanks, 3 million machine guns, and 7 million rifles.

⭐ American industry supplied its Allies of Great Britain, the Soviet Union, and France with more than half of their armaments.

⭐ More than 650,000 Jeeps were built during World War II.

⭐ The MI Garand rifle was considered the finest rifle in the war.

⭐ Because there was no time to construct a new building, the Lockheed corporation, an aircraft manufacturer, bought a brewery and converted it for making P-38 Lightning fighter planes.

Below: Navy dive-bombers being assembled. *Inset:* Detail from a World War II poster. *Opposite:* Women learning welding skills.

In September 1940, when told that Japan was planning to go to war against the United States, Admiral Isoroku Yamamoto, who had visited the United States and seen its industry, said, "If I am told to fight regardless of the consequences, I shall run wild for the first six months or a year, but I have utterly no confidence for the second or third year."

He had good reason for his statement. While millions of American men were leaving their jobs and marching into military bases, millions of women were filling those now-vacant positions on the assembly line and in other companies all across America. Their labor would supply not only their husbands and brothers but also their Allies with everything they needed to wage war. One woman factory worker, in particular, became a legend. With a partner, Rosina D. Bonavita assembled in one shift an entire wing of a torpedo bomber, ramming in a record 3,345 rivets. This, and other herculean feats of production, caused her to become famous as "Rosie the Riveter."

Adm. Yamamoto died in battle before he saw his prediction come true, before he saw the sky over Japan become black with American warplanes, and its shores ringed with American ships. The American workers' war on the home front made the soldiers and sailors' successful war on the front lines possible.

Above: A poster depicting Rosie the Riveter.

QUICK FACTS

The B-17 bomber had a top speed of 310 miles an hour, a ceiling of 35,000 feet, a range of 2,000 miles, and could carry 15,200 pounds of bombs. 12,731 were built.

The B-24 Liberator had a top speed of 310 miles an hour, a ceiling of 30,000 feet, a range of 3,100 miles, and could carry 15,200 pounds of bombs. 18,313 were built. More B-24s were built than any other U.S. warplane.

The bombers used a precision optical device called a Norden Bombsight. It was so good, it was claimed a bombadier could "drop a bomb into a pickle barrel" from 25,000 feet.

The B-17 first saw action with Britain's Royal Air Force, but the RAF rejected it because they thought it was too slow and clumsy.

The Germans used the first jet fighters in the war, among them the Messerschmitt Me-262. But they came too late to change the course of the war.

North Africa and Sicily had been liberated. Allied Armies were fighting their way up Italy toward Rome. At the same time, Allied planners wanted to land in France and liberate northern Europe. But first they had to defeat the German Air Force—the *Luftwaffe*—and destroy the factories that made everything Germany needed to wage war. This was the assignment of the fighters and bombers of the U.S. Army Air Forces.

One such raid was launched against Schweinfurt, Germany, on August 17, 1943. The U.S. Eighth Air Force sent 230 B-17 and B-24 bombers to destroy the factories in Germany's biggest ball bearing plant. They were attacked by German fighters all the way from the English Channel to the target, where antiaircraft gunners opened up on them. The Americans lost thirty-six B-17s and B-24s (with ten men on each plane) in the raid and took hundreds of casualties on bombers that managed to limp back to base. The attack did cause a temporary thirty-eight percent decline in production, but it was not enough. A second raid took place on October 14 and was later called "Black Thursday" because 65 of the 291 bombers were shot down and 17 others sustained damage that was beyond repair. It was one of the most expensive air attacks of the war because so many lives were lost.

Before returning home, American airmen initially had to fly twenty-five missions. Later in the war that number was raised to thirty-five, then fifty. Chances of surviving intact were slim. Some planes exploded when an anti-aircraft shell burst inside the plane or a stream of bullets hit the fuel tank. In such cases no one got out. Other bombers lost one, then two, and occasionally three engines. A few of them returned to England. In others the crews had to bail out over enemy territory and, if they landed safely, became POWs. On raids deep into Germany the air armada took tremendous losses, up to fifty percent overall. Despite the high cost, the bombers and fighters accomplished many of their goals. By the time the Allied armies reached Germany's borders in late 1944, the Luftwaffe had been virtually destroyed and most of Germany's factories had been turned to rubble.

Left: A B-24 Liberator bomber destroyed during a raid.
Opposite: A B-17 Flying Fortress bomber crew returning from a mission.

QUICK FACTS

★ The code name for the Manhattan Project was Trinity.

★ 190,000 people worked on the Manhattan Project.

★ The Manhattan Project cost 2 billion dollars.

★ The project was so secret that Vice President Harry S Truman learned of it only after he became president.

★ The atomic bomb at Alamogordo had the explosive power equivalent to 15,000–20,000 tons of regular bomb explosive.

On August 2, 1939, Albert Einstein, the internationally famous physicist who was forced to flee Germany because he was Jewish, wrote a letter to President Roosevelt. He had heard that it was possible to use uranium in a chain reaction to release incredible amounts of energy. Because scientists in Nazi Germany were researching methods to do this, Einstein was afraid that they would create an "extremely powerful bomb of a new type . . . [that when] carried by boat and exploded in a port might well destroy the whole port together with some of the surrounding territory . . ."

Einstein's letter caused President Roosevelt to create the Manhattan Project, the code name for the joint U.S./Great Britain effort to build an atomic bomb. It was placed under U.S. Army control and was administered by Brigadier General Leslie R. Groves. Dr. J. Robert Oppenheimer was the leader of the many distinguished scientists who worked on the bomb.

They worked under the strictest of secrecy—and in a race against time, because they were never sure how close German scientists were to making their own bomb. Fortunately Germany surrendered before its bomb could be made. Even though they were all allies fighting Nazi Germany, democratic America and Great Britain did not tell Josef Stalin about the atomic bomb until just before it was used against Japan. They did not trust the Communist Soviet Union because for years it had called for worldwide Communist revolution in all non-Communist countries. It didn't matter. Stalin had a spy in the Manhattan Project, Klaus Fuchs, who was able to tell him everything. Fuchs' information helped Stalin to later build a Soviet atomic bomb. On July 16, 1945, the U.S. Army exploded an experimental bomb at Alamogordo, New Mexico. An eyewitness recorded, "No man-made force of such tremendous power has ever occurred before."

It had taken a war to open the atomic age for mankind.

Left: The security checkpoint at Los Alamos, New Mexico.
Opposite: The Little Boy atomic bomb.

QUICK FACTS

★ The official name for the invasion was Operation Overlord.

★ The purpose was to free France from Nazi tyranny.

★ 3 million men, 5,300 ships, and 12,000 airplanes participated. Allied casualties at the end of D-Day were estimated at 4,900 men.

★ The U.S. Army landed at beaches code-named Omaha and Utah. The British and Canadian Armies landed at beaches code-named Gold, Juno, and Sword.

★ The invasion site had no harbors so 2 artificial ones, called Mulberry Harbors, were created and towed to the beaches.

★ To confuse the enemy the Allies dropped dummy paratroopers filled with firecrackers behind the German units who were guarding the invasion beaches.

Above: Gen. Dwight D. Eisenhower.
Opposite: Soldiers wading ashore on D-Day.

During the battles in Sicily and mainland Italy the American and British war planners were deciding which was the best spot in northern France to land an invasion force that would be able to drive quickly into Germany. There were many challenges. The landing beaches had to be within range of protective Allied fighter planes based in England. They had to be in an area where defense fortifications were weak or incomplete. And, perhaps hardest of all, the invasion had to be where the enemy would least expect one. The place chosen was the shore of Normandy, France.

On June 6, 1944, the American and British armies landed. This landing was not only the biggest amphibious operation in history but the most thoroughly planned and practiced. In preparation for going ashore on D-Day, 170,000 soldiers, British and Canadian and American, participated in exercises from January through May of 1944. Every one of them knew what was expected of him and what he could expect in the way of German resistance. They knew that Hitler had erected defenses called the Atlantic Wall to stop them. The Atlantic Wall consisted of reinforced concrete forts, trenches, minefields, and anti-landing craft devices of all kinds, and it was backed up by *panzer* (tank) divisions and was manned by battle-hardened Nazis.

The Allied soldiers were carried across the English Channel by ship or plane and were commanded by the best officers their countries could produce. They would be supported by more than 5,000 planes, including four-engine bombers and all types of fighters, dropping 500-pound bombs or firing rockets or strafing with .50-caliber machine guns, and by over 2,000 fighting ships firing cannon on the German positions. The smallest cannon shells were five inches in diameter, the largest were fourteen inches across.

But in the end success or failure of the invasion depended on these troops. If they were adequately trained and equipped, if their spirits were high, if they were tough enough, determined enough, they would accept their losses and continue to attack until they prevailed. If not, they would be pushed back into the sea from whence they had come. General Eisenhower met as many of the troops as he could during their training to see for himself how they were doing. Eisenhower, observing firing-range practice of

Above: Men and supplies being off-loaded onto a D-Day beach.

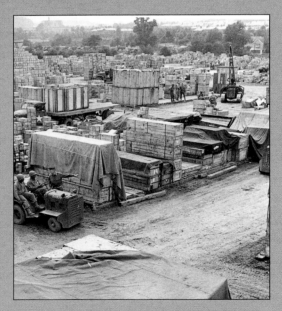

Above: An English ballpark used to store supplies for D-Day.

Opposite: The French city of St. Lo after its liberation by the Americans.

one outfit, told Sergeant Weldon Kratzer, "Sergeant, I'm impressed with your marksmanship. You sure know your Kentucky windage [the ability to judge how wind will affect the path of a bullet]."

"General Eisenhower," Kratzer replied, "I'm from Virginia. I use Virginia windage." Eisenhower met many men like Sgt. Kratzer.

At one of the landing sites, Omaha Beach, the incoming fire from the German machine guns and cannons was horrendous. Sergeant John R. Slaughter recalled, "There were dead men floating in the water and there were live men acting dead, letting the tide take them in." They needed leaders to get them off the killing field that was the beach. In Sergeant William Lewis's case, "Lieutenant Leo Van de Voort said, 'Let's go . . . there ain't no use staying here, we're all going to get killed!' The first thing he did was to run up to a gun emplacement and throw a grenade in the embrasure. He returned with five or six prisoners. So then we thought, if he can do that, why can't we. That's how we got off the beach."

On D-Day these men fought some of the toughest soldiers in the German Army, and beat them. Less than a year later, these soldiers that Hitler scorned would win the war against Nazi Germany and end his dream of "A Thousand-Year Reich."

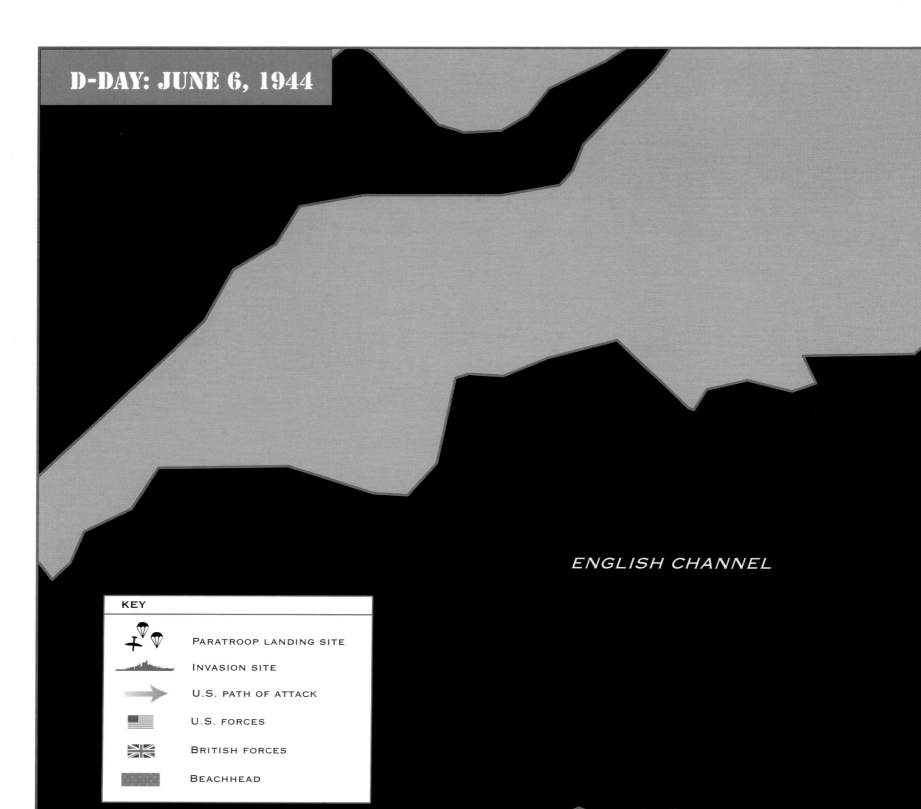

D-DAY: JUNE 6, 1944

ENGLISH CHANNEL

KEY

Paratroop landing site

Invasion site

U.S. path of attack

U.S. forces

British forces

Beachhead

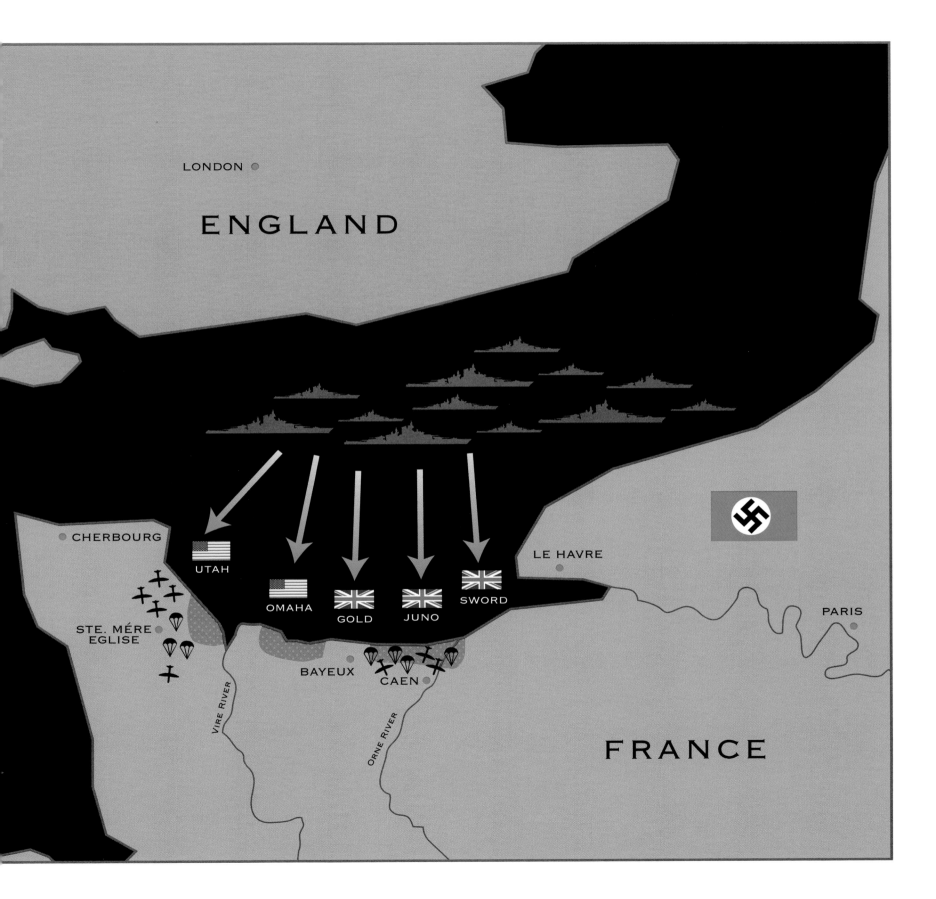

LONDON

ENGLAND

CHERBOURG

UTAH

OMAHA

GOLD

JUNO

SWORD

LE HAVRE

STE. MÉRE
EGLISE

BAYEUX

CAEN

PARIS

VIRE RIVER

ORNE RIVER

FRANCE

QUICK FACTS

QUICK FACTS

⭐ The Japanese used 9 aircraft carriers and 473 Navy planes in the battle.

⭐ The U.S. Navy used 15 aircraft carriers and 956 airplanes.

⭐ The Japanese lost 3 aircraft carriers and more than 400 planes and pilots.

⭐ The U.S. Navy lost 49 aircraft in battle and 80 more that ran out of fuel on the flight back to the carriers.

⭐ U.S. Navy submarines sank 2 Japanese aircraft carriers.

⭐ Over 160 U.S. Navy pilots and bombardiers who made night landings in the ocean were rescued. Only 49 men were lost.

Above: An aircraft carrier flight crew works to clear away a Hellcat fighter plane that's crash-landed.
Opposite: A burning Japanese dive-bomber vainly tries to crash-land on a U.S. Navy aircraft carrier.

The offensive in the Central Pacific continued in the summer of 1944 with the American invasion of the Marianas Islands of Saipan, Guam, and Tinian. These islands were needed as bases for the new gigantic B-29 Superfortress bombers that were to bomb Japan, which was still fighting relentlessly in the Pacific.

On June 15, 1944, the first island, Saipan, was invaded. While the one Army and two Marine divisions battled the Japanese defenders, the Imperial Japanese Navy was preparing a coordinated attack that would destroy the U.S. Pacific Fleet once and for all.

On June 19 the greatest aircraft-carrier battle of the war occurred. All day the fighter pilots on both sides held midair duels as their fellow pilots in dive-bombers and torpedo planes tried to sink each other's ships. This time the U.S. Navy pilots were both better trained and were in better planes than at Midway. The result was even more impressive. So many Japanese aircrafts were shot out of the sky that one Navy pilot said it was like "an old-time turkey shoot."

The battle lasted into the evening and almost ended in disaster for the U.S. Navy. The pilots returning from their last mission were flying in total darkness. They were tired, some were wounded, some had damaged planes, and all were low on gas. Vice Admiral Marc Mitscher, commander of the aircraft carrier task force, ordered, "Turn on the lights." It was a dangerous decision. The carriers would be perfect targets for submarine attack. No admiral in the Japanese or German Navy would risk his ships to save a few men. But Vice Adm. Mitscher *was* willing to take that risk. Hundreds of planes successfully landed. Those that ditched in the ocean were rescued by the escort ships. One pilot who crash-landed in the Pacific, and was feared lost, was the beloved Lieutenant Commander William R. "Killer" Kane of the aircraft carrier *Enterprise.* Two days after the battle, a U.S. destroyer sailed close to the *Enterprise* and signaled a "ransom" message, "How much ice cream is Killer Kane worth?"

The Great Marianas Turkey Shoot, known officially as the Battle of the Philippine Sea, broke the back of Japanese naval aviation.

QUICK FACTS

⭐ Author Ernest Hemingway was a war correspondent in World War II and was with the troops that freed Paris.

⭐ General Dietrich von Choltitz, German commander of Paris, had been ordered by Hitler to destroy Paris. But Gen. von Choltitz disobeyed Hitler's order. He knew that Germany was losing the war and he did not want to be remembered by history as the man who destroyed one of the most beautiful cities in the world.

⭐ On Liberation Night, Paris turned on all the street and monument lights and for the first time since September 1, 1939, it once again became "the City of Light."

As the Allied armies surged out of Normandy and started racing across France in pursuit of the retreating German Army, Gen. Eisenhower faced a dilemma. Soon his armies would be in position to take the capital of France. Liberating Paris had tremendous symbolic importance, both to the American and British and especially to their ally, the Free French forces under General Charles de Gaulle. The Germans had only a few garrison troops in Paris for security, and some small combat units were in Paris and its suburbs and these soldiers wanted to retreat to Germany. Yet, militarily, taking Paris would be very costly. Once the Allies captured the city, vital supplies of food and fuel that their own armies needed would have to be given to the five million people of Paris. Gen. Eisenhower hoped to delay his day of decision as long as possible.

But when the French Resistance in Paris rose in revolt against the small German garrison, Gen. Eisenhower was forced to act. He ordered his troops to liberate Paris before the German Army could crush the rebellion and obey Hitler's orders to burn Paris to the ground.

General Jacque LeClerc's French 2nd Armored Division raced with Major General Raymond O. Barton's U.S. 4th Infantry Division to be the first into Paris. For some, like Tech Sergeant Milt Shenton, who would become the first American to enter the city, Paris ". . . was a poor boy's dream come true." For others like Private Willie Hancock, it was ". . . just another big German-held city on the road to Berlin and home."

As the sun was setting on August 24, 1944, Captain Raymond Dronne of the French 2nd Armored Division crossed the Porte d'Italie and became the first soldier to enter Paris. With the exception of scattered skirmishes, the German Army had left, surrendering Paris without a fight. The morning of the 25th was Liberation Day, and like their fellow soldiers in the French 2nd Armored Division, Tech Sgt. Shenton and the other Americans who entered the city were mobbed by an ecstatic population.

Left: **Home away from home.**
Opposite: **U.S. soldiers in a victory parade down the Champs-Élysées in Paris, France.**

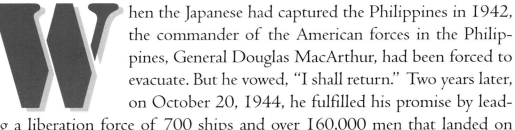

QUICK FACTS

★ The Philippines have almost 7,100 islands.

★ The Philippines were a U.S. territory. It was granted independence in 1946.

★ The escort carriers were nicknamed Jeep Carriers and Baby Flat-Tops.

★ The Japanese used a terrible new weapon for the first time in the Philippines, the *kamikaze* (divine wind). Kamikazes were bomb-carrying suicide warplanes. The pilots in the planes had just enough gas to reach their target, usually a warship. The pilot would then try to crash into it.

★ The Battle of Leyte Gulf was the largest naval battle in history. It lasted 4 days and 282 warships fought in it.

When the Japanese had captured the Philippines in 1942, the commander of the American forces in the Philippines, General Douglas MacArthur, had been forced to evacuate. But he vowed, "I shall return." Two years later, on October 20, 1944, he fulfilled his promise by leading a liberation force of 700 ships and over 160,000 men that landed on the central Philippine island of Leyte.

The Japanese fought back hard, knowing that this was their last chance to win the war. They came closest to victory in the Battle of Leyte Gulf on October 25, 1944. Two Japanese fleets had succeeded in luring away most of the U.S. Navy ships. A third Japanese fleet with five battleships, ten heavy cruisers, two light cruisers, and fifteen destroyers sailed toward the invasion site and opened fire on the small force of tiny escort carriers, destroyers and destroyer escorts that guarded the vulnerable beachhead. The U.S. naval force was woefully outmatched. But the courage and fighting spirit of the American sailors and aviators in the face of the larger Japanese ships and guns was amazing. Sinking Navy ships continued shooting at the Japanese battlewagons. Planes that had no more bombs or torpedoes made dummy attacks. Just when it looked as if everything would be lost for the Americans, the Japanese ships broke off the action and reversed course. The Americans had won.

Lt. Commander Robert Copeland, commander of the destroyer escort USS *Samuel B. Roberts*, said later it was "a fight against overwhelming odds from which survival could not be expected. In the face of this knowledge the men zealously manned their stations wherever they might be, and fought and worked with such calmness, courage, and efficiency that no higher honor could be conceived than to command such a group of men."

There was much hard fighting left on the Philippines, but the Japanese fleet was never again a threat.

Left: Gen. Douglas MacArthur (center) wading ashore on the Philippine Island of Leyte.
Opposite: A soldier rescuing a shell-shocked girl during the liberation of Manila, Philippines.

QUICK FACTS

⭐ The B-29 bomber had a top speed of 358 miles an hour, a ceiling of 30,000 feet, and a range of 5,333 miles, and could carry 20,000 pounds of bombs.

⭐ The B-29 was the first airplane with a fully pressurized cabin.

⭐ Except for the tail gun, the B-29's machine gun defense system was operated by remote control.

⭐ On the night of March 9–10, 1945, 334 B-29s dropped over 2,000 tons of firebombs on Tokyo. The resulting fire-storm destroyed a quarter of the city, including 20 important war-industry targets, killed almost 85,000 Japanese civilians, and injured tens of thousands more. It was one of the most destructive raids in World War II.

With the Americans in possession of Saipan, Tinian, and Guam, the air war against the Japanese homeland could begin.

Originally, the new B-29 Superfortress bombers attacked industrial sites the same way the B-17s and B-24s did over Germany. But the bombings weren't as successful as they needed to be. Army Air Force General Curtis LeMay took command in February 1945 and changed the way the B-29s would attack. He used as his model the way Britain's Royal Air Force used its bombers, with some changes. Instead of high-level flights, the B-29s would come in low over their targets. Instead of high-explosive bombs, the B-29s would carry firebombs. In addition, more bombings would be at night rather than during the day.

This new stage in the air war started in the middle of February 1945. The results were greater than anyone ever expected. Because most Japanese buildings were made of wood, entire cities were destroyed. On March 9, 1945, 334 B-29s attacked Tokyo in the greatest firebomb raid ever. By mid-June the industrial centers of five other major Japanese cities were wrecked.

Everyone knew that Japanese civilians would be hurt in these attacks. No one liked it. The goal was to destroy Japan's industrial might, not its civilians. But the Japanese leaders kept the civilians near the war-industry factories, refusing to let them leave even after American planes dropped leaflets warning of an upcoming attack.

And still, the Japanese military leaders refused to surrender. They would not allow themselves to lose face even at the cost of hundreds of thousands of civilian lives. The attacks continued. It would take the terrible use of atomic weapons finally to force Japan's surrender.

Left: U.S. Navy bombers dropping bombs on Japan.
Opposite: Crew members of the B-29 bomber Waddy's Wagon playfully mimic the nose art of their bomber.

QUICK FACTS

⭐ 3 German Armies with 25 divisions attacked 6 American divisions.

⭐ Over 1,000,000 men took part in the battle. Half the field artillery battalions in Bastogne were African-American units.

⭐ When the German Army surrounded the town of Bastogne and ordered the Americans to surrender, Brigadier General Anthony McAuliffe refused. His answer, "Nuts!", made him famous.

⭐ English-speaking German commandos wearing U.S. Army uniforms spread chaos behind the American lines.

⭐ Lt. Gen. Patton launched a counter-attack with 3 divisions within 48 hours of the German attack.

A s 1944 came to a close, it looked as though Germany was running out of resources with which to fight. The Americans thought the Germans would give up before the New Year began, but at 5 A.M. on December 16, Hitler launched a major offensive that came as a complete surprise. In the Ardennes Forest of Belgium the Germans broke through thinly held American lines and drove on toward the English Channel, destroying two American divisions. The Germans put more men, tanks, airplanes, and other firepower into the offensive than they had four years earlier when they attacked the French Army. It became the biggest battle that the U.S. Army had ever fought.

The Germans thought they had succeeded in their goal of dividing the Allies and were about to drive the American, Canadian, and British troops out of Europe.

But here, there, and everywhere throughout the battle zone individual Americans began to resist. At Elsenborn Ridge, Sergeant Arnold Parish of the 2nd Infantry recalled, "We were helpless and all alone and there was nothing we could do, so I prayed to God. . . . The time went by very slow as I tried to keep warm but that wasn't possible so I thought about my mother and hoped she didn't know where I was or what I was doing. I was glad I was not married." When the German infantry attacked, supported by tanks, Sgt. Parish thought that perhaps it was the end of the world. But within seconds he and his platoon were firing back. The German attack was repulsed.

At Bastogne, the surrounded troops of the 10th Armored and the 101st Airborne Divisions held out until relieved by fresh troops. At St. Vith the Germans were held up for days. Throughout the Ardennes the GIs dug in and badly disrupted the German timetable. By the end of the month the Germans had been thrown back and were on the defensive. It was a great victory brought about by ordinary men who wanted nothing more than to go back home, but first they had a job to do.

Left: Paratroopers landing in Ardennes.
Opposite: U.S. Army Sherman tanks.

QUICK FACTS

⭐ Iwo Jima is a pork chop–shaped island of about 8 square miles. Mount Suribachi is an extinct volcano.

⭐ Rosenthal's famous photograph is actually of the second flag-raising. A smaller flag had been raised earlier, but was judged too small to be seen from the beach.

⭐ The Japanese commander on Iwo Jima copied the defense plan used by the Japanese commander of Tarawa and honeycombed the island with bunkers and pillboxes. In one spot 1,000 yards long and 200 yards deep the Marines destroyed over 800 Japanese pillboxes.

⭐ The fighting was among the toughest in the war. In one day 5 Marines of the 5th Division won America's highest military decoration, the Medal of Honor, an extraordinary achievement.

In order to carry out the planned invasion of Japan, the United States forces needed to have land airfields as close as possible to the Japanese homeland. Iwo Jima was targeted for invasion for this purpose.

On February 19, 1945, 30,000 Marines landed on Iwo Jima. The planners of the operation figured that it would take a week, possibly two, to capture the island. Instead it took thirty-six days of hard, bitter fighting. The Marines discovered that the Japanese troops had done the same thing as the defenders of Tarawa had. Iwo Jima was honeycombed with underground bunkers, pillboxes, and tunnels. Marines would think they had destroyed a bunker and move. Then suddenly they'd be attacked from behind by Japanese soldiers who had used a tunnel to reoccupy the bunker.

As fighting continued and more and more men fell, questions were asked whether taking the island was worth the cost. Then on March 4, Lieutenant Raymond Malo made an emergency landing with his damaged B-29 on one of Iwo Jima's airfields while it was still under fire by Japanese mortars. He was the first of many pilots who got their crippled airplanes to Iwo Jima safely. As one grateful pilot said, "Whenever I land on this island, I thank God and the men who fought for it." Secretary of the Navy James Forrestal said of what the Marines suffered on Iwo Jima, "I can never again see a United States Marine without feeling a reverence."

On February 23, 1945, the U.S. Marines reached the top of Mount Suribachi and raised the U.S. flag. Associated Press photographer Joe Rosenthal took a photograph of the event. It became the most famous photograph of the century. At first he wasn't happy with the photo because only two of the Marines' faces were even visible. But as a symbol for the citizen soldiers who were fighting in the war, it was unmatched.

Left: U.S. Marines receiving communion.
Opposite: Joe Rosenthal's photograph of the flag-raising on Mount Suribachi.

Below: Soldiers treat the wounds of a young boy.

The Rhine River was the last natural defense barrier that could stop the Allies—no enemy forces had crossed the German river since Julius Caesar in 55 B.C. On March 7, 1945, GIs captured the Ludendorff Bridge, which spanned the Rhine River at Remagen, Germany. Hitler ordered it destroyed. German aircraft and artillery, floating mines, and other devices were put on the mission. Meanwhile, American engineers had been working night and day to erect pontoon crossings, built on rafts held in place by triple anchors. The damaged bridge collapsed ten days later, but by then the pontoon bridges nearby were up and running. The pontoons were 969 feet long, the longest floating bridges ever constructed. A tank could cross on them every two minutes. During the first seven days 2,500 vehicles did so. Building these pontoon bridges was a superb feat of engineering.

The unit that captured the bridge was typically all-American. The officer who led the men over the bridge to the far bank was Lieutenant Karl Timmermann, whose father had been in the American occupation force in 1919 and married a girl from Remagen, then brought her back to his native Nebraska, where Timmermann was born. Sergeants Joe DeLisio, Joe Petrenecsik, and Alex Drabik were with him as he dashed across the bridge in the face of mortars, machine gun fire, hand grenades, and German explosives meant to blow the bridge. Engineers came right behind them, searching for demolitions and tearing out electrical wires. Once they were across, Timmermann pointed to the hill just ahead, called the Erpeler Ley, and told platoon leader Lieutenant Emmet "Jim" Burrows and his men to take it, "You know, Jim, the old Fort Benning stuff [where they had trained]; take the high ground and hold it." Burrows later said, "Taking Remagen and crossing the bridge were a breeze compared with climbing that hill."

The names of some of the citizen soldiers who took the bridge were Chinchar, Samele, Massie, Wegener, Jensen. They were Italian, Czech, Norwegian, German, Russian. They were a diverse unit with one mission, a mission accomplished.

Opposite: Soldiers in an assault boat crossing the Rhine River.

QUICK FACTS

⭐ *The Diary of Anne Frank* tells the story of Anne and her German-Jewish family, victims of Nazi persecution. Anne died in the Bergen-Belsen concentration camp in March 1945. Her father, Otto, found his daughter's diary and had it published. In 1977 a statue of Anne Frank was unveiled near the place where she and her family hid in Amsterdam, the Netherlands.

⭐ Hitler's Final Solution also included Poles, Russians, Gypsies, Serbs, Catholics, Jehovah's Witnesses, the handicapped, and homosexuals.

⭐ 11 million civilians, including 6 million Jews, were believed killed in the Final Solution.

⭐ Reparations—payments—to survivors or their heirs continue to this day.

⭐ German industrialist and Nazi Party member Oskar Schindler saved the lives of 1,300 Jews. His story was made into the film *Schindler's List*.

⭐ The Holocaust is also known in Yiddish as *Churban* (the Destruction) and in Hebrew as *Shoah* (the Catastrophe).

In his book *Mein Kampf*, Adolf Hitler, a racist who hated Jews in particular, stated that when he became ruler of Germany, he would rid it of all the Jews. He blamed German Jews for the defeat Germany suffered in World War I; he claimed they were subhuman creatures, and worse. Before 1933, no one took him seriously because his statements were so extreme as to be unbelievable. But when he became chancellor in 1933, Hitler wasted no time starting his insane plan. First he passed a series of laws that stripped the Jews of almost all rights. In 1935 the Nuremberg Racial Laws stripped the Jews of German citizenship. On the night of November 9, 1938, synagogues and Jewish shops, businesses and homes were burned or vandalized. *Kristallnacht* ("Night of Broken Glass") was the first violent pogrom in Western Europe that marked a new stage of the Nazi campaign against the Jews. Secretly Hitler had ordered the creation of concentration camps where the Jews would be isolated. In countries that Germany had captured, Jews were identified and shipped to the concentration camps.

The Wannsee Conference on January 20, 1942 formally established Hitler's "final solution for the Jewish question" for the purpose of killing Jews. Death camps were built in Dachau, Belsen, Buchenwald, Treblinka, Auschwitz, and hundreds of other places in Germany and Nazi-occupied territory in the east. Upon arriving at a concentration camp, the crippled and the elderly were separated from the others and put to death. Babies were seized from the arms of their mothers and quickly killed, too. The methods were diabolical in their variety. Some victims were forced to dig their own graves, then they were shot and killed. Special trucks, built with exhaust pipes that would funnel poisonous engine exhaust fumes into the trailer, would drive down roads until the passengers in the trailer were dead. Gas chambers designed as large showers killed many more. More than five million people were gassed and cremated.

News of the Nazi atrocities leaked out, but most people refused to believe that anyone could be so monstrous. The tales of mass killings, biological experiments on human guinea pigs and the use of human skin for

Left: Cyanide pellets used to gas concentration camp inmates.
Opposite: Female inmates at Belsen concentration camp.

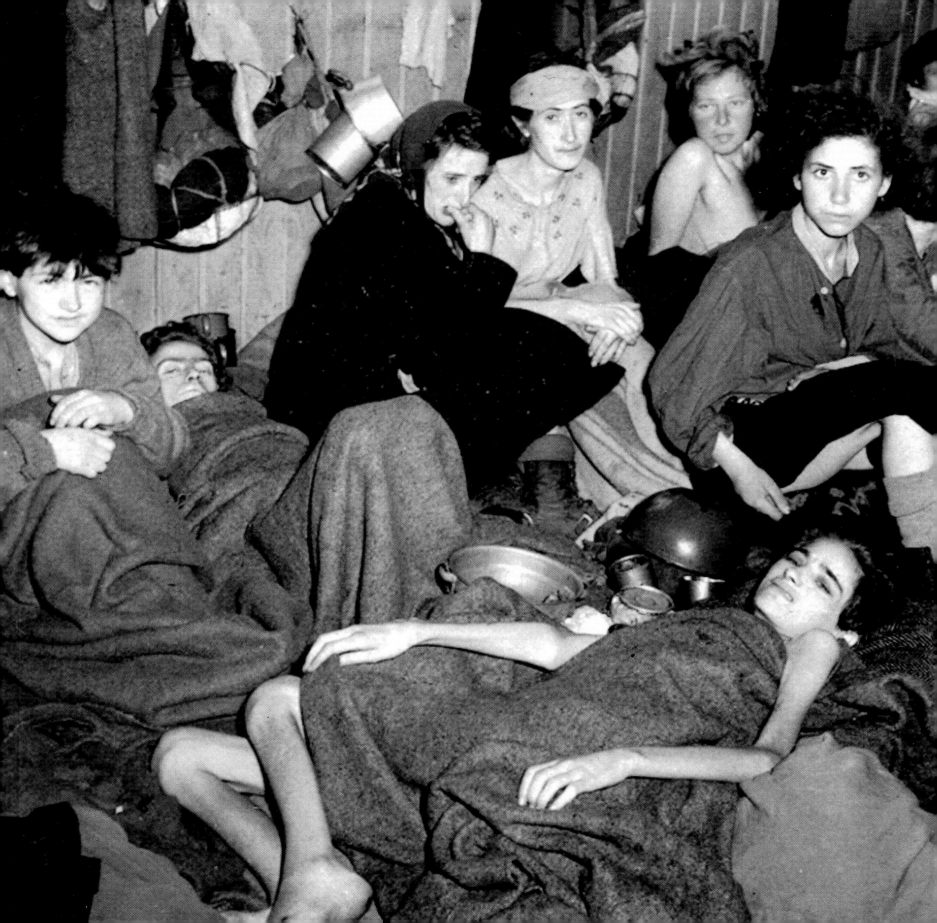

lamp shades were simply unimaginable. The full horror of what the Nazis had done was finally revealed when the Russian Army liberated Auschwitz in Poland, and the British and American Armies freed concentration camps in western Germany.

Major Richard Winters voiced the emotions of so many of his fellow soldiers when he said of the sight at Dachau, "Now I know why I am here."

Below, left: Children in Auschwitz.
Below, right: A concentration camp inmate.

Opposite: A map showing most of the German concentration camps.

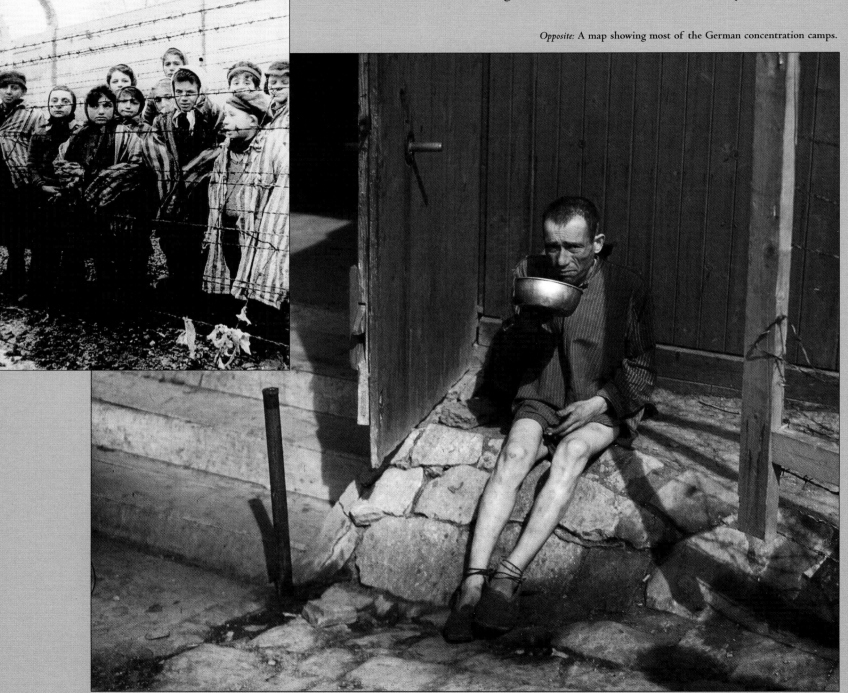

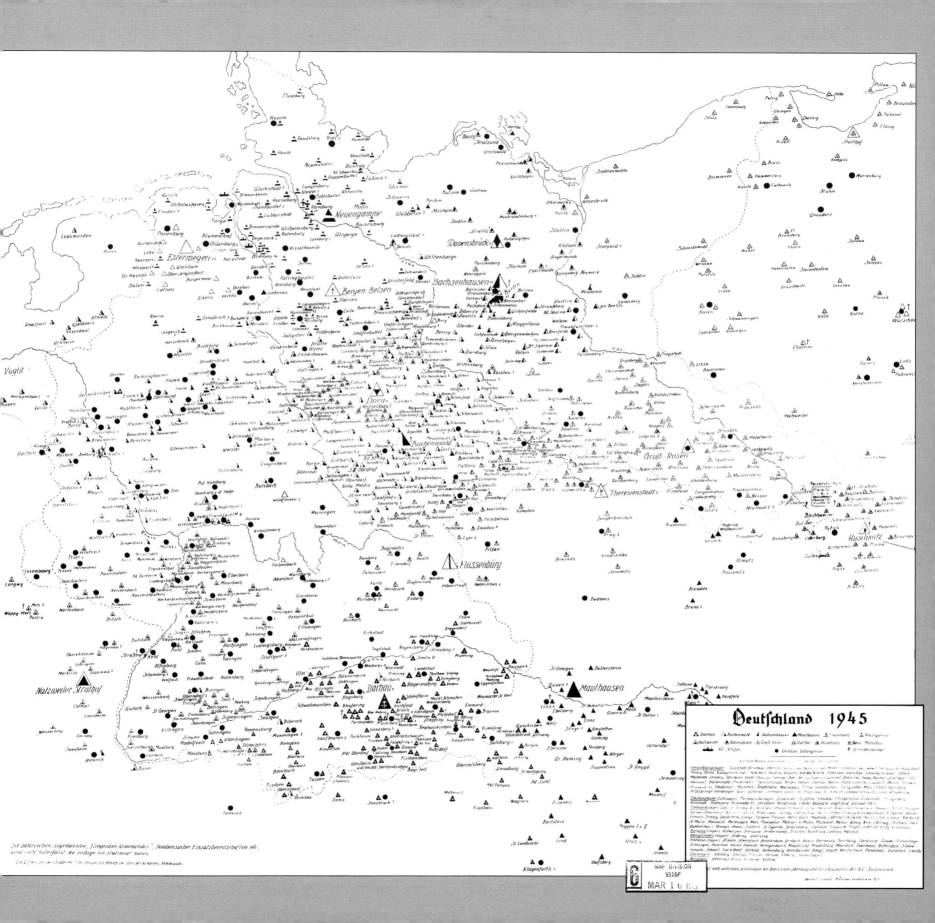

Deutschland 1945

In April 1945 organized German Army resistance was evaporating. With the Soviet Armies entering his shattered capital of Berlin, Hitler, deep in his bunker, ordered his soldiers to fight to the last man. Though some fanatic Nazis did, most German soldiers saw that continuing the battle was just a delusional fantasy.

Gen. Eisenhower's priority was the Allies' advance across the center of Germany, linking with the Soviet Army and cutting Germany in two. Because his troops were traveling so fast, he was concerned that his troops would literally run into the Russians and that both sides would mistakenly shoot at each other. To prevent that, Eisenhower drew a border along the Elbe River. There the American and British troops would stop and wait for their Russian allies.

On April 25, 1945, at Torgau, Germany, Lieutenant William D. Robinson of the First Army met a Red Army soldier. Germany had been divided! Immediately the Russians and the Americans began to celebrate. The Russians held a large red banner reading: OUR GREETINGS TO THE BRAVE TROOPS OF THE AMERICAN FIRST ARMY. Hundreds of Red Army soldiers found rowboats and rafts and crossed the Elbe to visit the American troops. A factory in Torgau produced harmonicas and accordions, so there was music and dancing.

First Army commander, General Courtney Hodges called his superior, General Omar Bradley, and told him the historic news. Gen. Bradley said, "Thanks, Courtney, thanks again for calling. We've been waiting a long time. . . ." Gen. Bradley hung up, opened a bottle of Coke, and circled Torgau on his wall map. The end of the war in Germany was less than two weeks away.

Left: U.S. and Soviet soldiers shaking hands.
Opposite: U.S. and Soviet soldiers celebrating their meeting near Torgau, Germany.

QUICK FACTS

⭐ The "V-E" in V-E Day stands for Victory in Europe.

⭐ At the end of the war, Gen. Eisenhower was in command of a total of 5,412,219 troops.

⭐ 135,576 U.S. soldiers would not return from the battlefields of western Europe.

⭐ Postwar Germany was divided into 4 military district zones of occupation, each one administered by one of the victorious Allies.

On April 30, 1945, shortly after the Allied troops had divided Germany at Torgau, Adolf Hitler committed suicide in his underground bunker in Berlin. At 2:41 A.M. on May 7, 1945, in a schoolhouse in Reims, France, the German government representatives signed the document of unconditional surrender, effective 11:01 P.M. on May 8. After almost six years, the war in Europe was finally over. CBS war correspondent Charles Collingwood, who observed the ceremony, said, "The mad dog of Europe was put out of the way, the strange monstrosity that was Nazi Germany had been beaten into submission." The Russians insisted on a second signing, in Berlin, which took place on May 8.

Corporal James Pemberton of the 103rd Division recalled, "The night of May 8, 1945, I was looking down from our cabin on the mountain at the Inn River Valley in Austria. It was black. And then the lights in Innsbruck went on. If you have not lived in darkness for months, shielding even a match light deep in a foxhole, you can't imagine the feeling."

Staff Sergeant Bruce Egger of G Company, 328th regiment, 26th Division, recalling the fighting through the fall and winter of 1944 and 1945, wrote much later, "We were miserable and cold and exhausted most of the time, were all scared to death. . . . But we were young and strong then, possessed of the marvelous resilience of youth, and for all the misery and fear and the hating every moment of it, the war was a great, if always terrifying, adventure. Not a man among us would want to go through it again, but we are all proud of having been so severely tested and found adequate. The only regret is for those of our friends who never returned."

Left: Gen. Dwight D. Eisenhower holds the pens used to sign the German surrender.
Opposite: V-E Day in Paris.

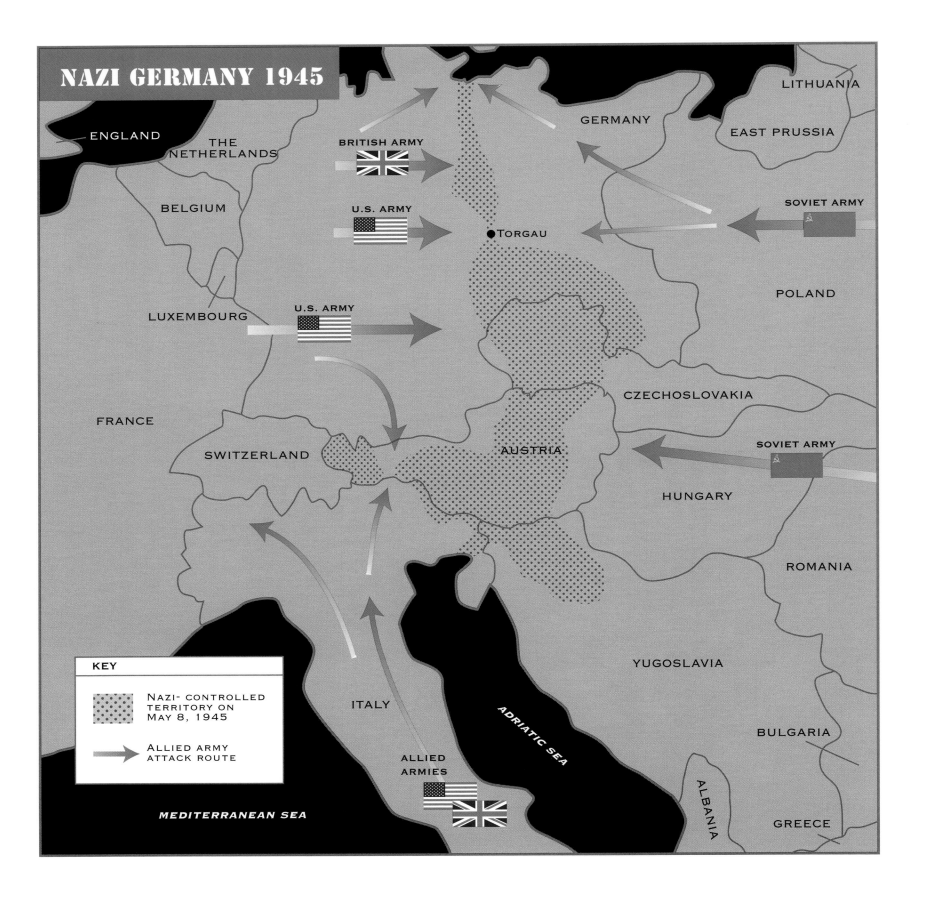

NAZI GERMANY 1945

ENGLAND

THE NETHERLANDS

BELGIUM

LUXEMBOURG

FRANCE

SWITZERLAND

ITALY

MEDITERRANEAN SEA

BRITISH ARMY

U.S. ARMY

U.S. ARMY

●Torgau

GERMANY

LITHUANIA

EAST PRUSSIA

SOVIET ARMY

POLAND

CZECHOSLOVAKIA

AUSTRIA

HUNGARY

SOVIET ARMY

ROMANIA

YUGOSLAVIA

BULGARIA

ALBANIA

GREECE

ADRIATIC SEA

ALLIED ARMIES

KEY

Nazi- controlled territory on May 8, 1945

Allied army attack route

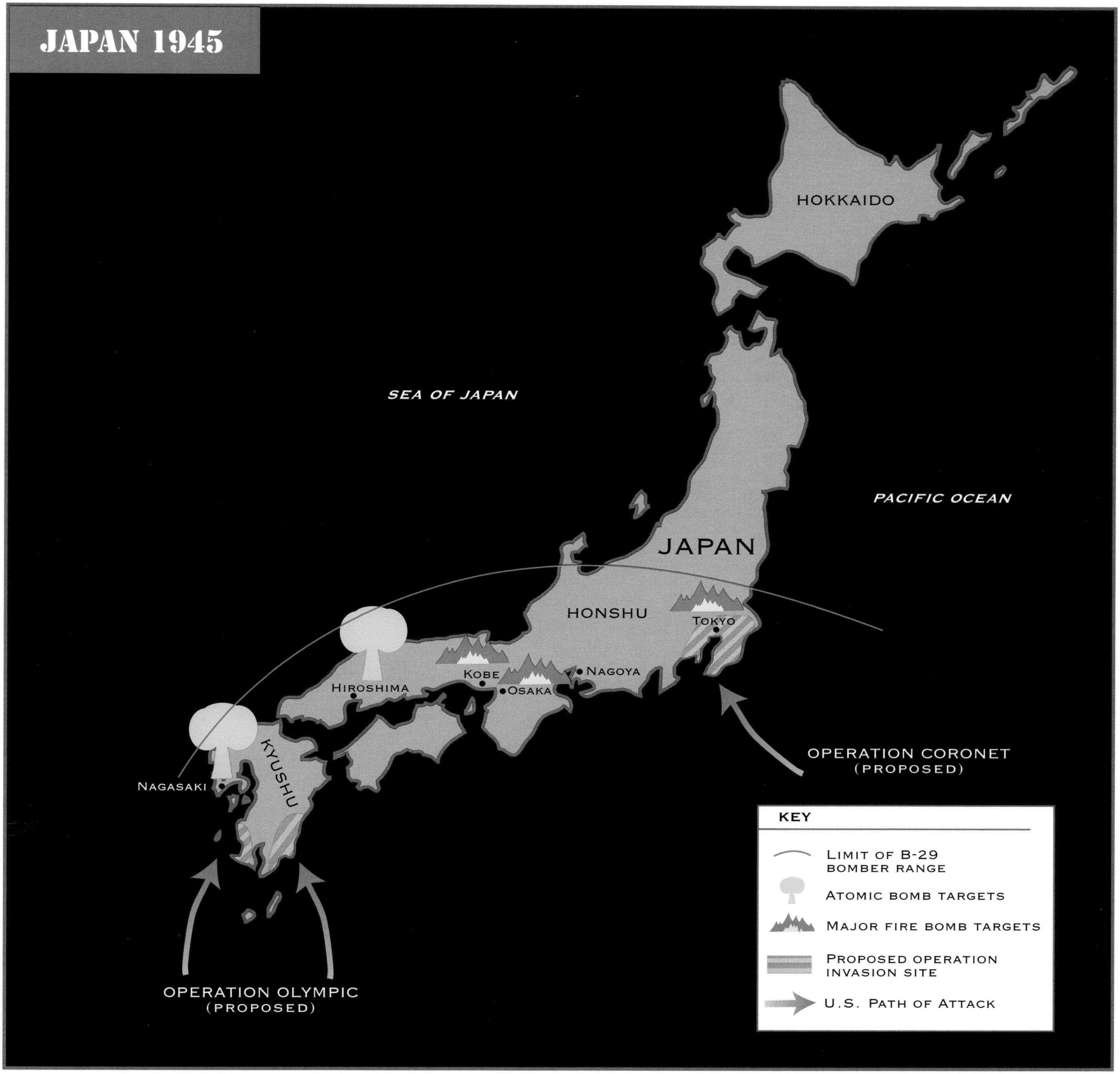

JAPAN 1945

HOKKAIDO

SEA OF JAPAN

PACIFIC OCEAN

JAPAN

HONSHU

Tokyo

Kobe

Osaka ● Nagoya

Hiroshima

KYUSHU

Nagasaki

OPERATION CORONET
(PROPOSED)

OPERATION OLYMPIC
(PROPOSED)

KEY

Limit of B-29
bomber range

Atomic bomb targets

Major fire bomb targets

Proposed operation
invasion site

U.S. Path of Attack

QUICK FACTS

★ The island of Okinawa is 459 square miles.

★ Lt. Gen. Simon Bolivar Buckner Jr., the commander of the U.S. invasion force, was killed in action in Okinawa. He was the highest-ranking commander to die in combat.

★ President Roosevelt died during the battle for Okinawa, on April 12. He was succeeded by Vice President Harry S Truman.

★ The U.S. Navy lost 36 ships during the battle, most by kamikaze attacks.

★ The U.S. invasion fleet had 1,300 ships and included 40 aircraft carriers, 18 battleships, and 200 destroyers.

★ Out of a total force of 120,000 men, 7,871 Japanese soldiers either were captured or surrendered. The others all died.

In April 1945 a combined Army-Marine force of 300,000 men attacked the southern Japanese island of Okinawa, which was honeycombed with caves. It was not possible for GIs and Marines simply to bypass the caves and push on, because the Japanese would emerge at their backs and subject them to withering fire. Offshore, some 350 kamikaze planes pounded the Navy. More U.S. sailors were killed or injured and more U.S. ships were sunk by kamikazes off Okinawa than in the Japanese attack on Pearl Harbor. American losses were right at the edge of being unacceptable. Altogether, American servicemen suffered 49,200 casualties, the heaviest American toll of the war in the Pacific.

The last Japanese stronghold did not fall until June, by which time Japanese losses were 110,071. When there were no Japanese soldiers left to fight, General Ushijima and his subordinates knelt in full-dress uniforms before their headquarters cave and committed *seppuku*. They had fought on in a hopeless situation, dooming tens of thousands of young Japanese and Americans to senseless deaths, then tried to absolve themselves through suicide. This bespoke a fanaticism never seen previously, a willingness on the part of Japan's military dictators to commit national suicide rather than to give up. All across America people wondered, *Isn't there another way to make them surrender?*

Right: A kamikaze pilot.
Far right: A kamikaze plane about to hit a U.S. Navy warship.
Opposite: Franklin receives a bomb hit from a Japanese plane.

QUICK FACTS

⭐ The code name for the Potsdam Conference was Terminal.

⭐ There was a total of 9 conferences. Only the conferences at Teheran, Iran, in 1943, at Yalta in the Crimea in 1944, and at Potsdam were attended by the leaders of the United States, Great Britain, and the Soviet Union.

⭐ At the Casablanca Conference between President Roosevelt and Prime Minister Churchill, in January 1943, Roosevelt publicly stated the U.S. and British position of "unconditional surrender." It meant that the U.S. and Great Britain would not make any deals with the Axis to end the war. The only choice the Axis had was to give up completely.

⭐ It was at the Yalta Conference that the United Nations organization was first discussed.

⭐ The atomic bomb was successfully tested during the Potsdam Conference.

Throughout the war the leaders of the Allies had held strategic conferences to decide how best to fight the Germans and Japanese. The Potsdam conference held in Potsdam, Germany, a suburb of Berlin, was the third, last, and longest meeting between the three major Allies—the United States, Great Britain, and the Soviet Union.

From July 17 to August 2, 1945, President Truman, Prime Minister Churchill, Soviet dictator Stalin, and their advisers met to discuss what would happen next in Europe and to plan for the next step in the war against Japan.

For Truman, it was his first time at a conference. The late President Roosevelt had attended the others. In the middle of the meeting Churchill had to leave. Great Britain had held an election and Churchill had lost. He was replaced by the new Prime Minister, Clement Attlee.

The Allies issued the Potsdam Declaration. In it, Nazism and all its institutions were made illegal. Poland was given new territory and a call was made for Japan to "unconditionally surrender."

At Potsdam the first cracks that would soon split the Allies began to appear. The most important difference that led to the later break between the Soviet Union and America and Great Britain was that the Soviet Union would allow only Communist governments to form in the countries it had liberated, including Poland, Czechoslovakia, Romania, Bulgaria, and Hungary. For the public, the leaders papered over their differences. But it was clear that when the conference ended that soon the Soviet Union would not be an ally of the United States and Great Britain, but possibly its enemy.

Left: British Prime Minister Winston Churchill, President Franklin Roosevelt, and Soviet Generalissimo Josef Stalin at Yalta, USSR.
Opposite: Generalissimo Josef Stalin, President Harry S Truman, and Prime Minister Winston Churchill at Potsdam, Germany.

QUICK FACTS

⭐ The bomb dropped on Hiroshima was called Little Boy. It was made of uranium. It was about 14 feet long and 5 feet in diameter. It weighed just under 10,000 pounds.

⭐ The bomb dropped on Nagasaki was called Fat Man. It used plutonium, which was more powerful than uranium.

⭐ Japan is the only country in the world ever to be attacked by atomic weapons. At least 140,000 people in Hiroshima and 75,000 in Nagasaki died from the blast and radiation sickness.

⭐ Both bombs had tail parachutes. This would slow the descent of the bomb, giving the B-29s time to get away safely.

⭐ The Soviet Union declared war on Japan on August 8, 1945, and invaded Japanese-held Manchuria.

By August 1945, Japan was defeated, but it refused to surrender. Operations Coronet and Olympic, the invasion of Japan, were ready to be launched, but everyone was reluctant to see them given the go-ahead. Gen. Douglas MacArthur, who would command the invasion, predicted that it would "cost over a million casualties to American forces alone."

Something had to be done to shock sense into the minds of the Japanese military leaders. But that "something" would have to be powerful indeed. President Truman knew he had a weapon with unimagined power. He just hoped that it would have the effect needed. It was the atomic bomb. He ordered the only two atomic bombs in the world to be flown from the United States to the B-29 air base on Saipan for use against Japan.

The first target was the city of Hiroshima on the island of Honshu. Colonel Paul W. Tibbetts Jr. piloted the B-29 *Enola Gay*, which carried the first atomic bomb. On August 6, 1945, at 8:15 A.M., it was released over Hiroshima. In a single blast, the city was destroyed. The world had a new image of war: a gigantic, terrifying mushroom cloud.

President Truman called upon the Japanese government to surrender, but the Japanese high command still refused. Three days later, on August 9, at 11:01 A.M., *Bock's Car*, the B-29 piloted by Major Charles W. Sweeney, dropped the second atomic bomb. Its target was the city of Nagasaki, on the island of Kyushu. Sweeny, who had witnessed the attack on Hiroshima, later said the "entire horizon burst into a superbrilliant white with an intense flash—more intense than Hiroshima."

On August 15, in the first public speech a Japanese emperor had ever made, Emperor Hirohito told the nation that the government was going to surrender. At long last World War II was truly over.

Left: A watch found at Hiroshima showing the time of the atomic bomb blast: 8:15 A.M.
Opposite: The atomic bomb attack on Nagasaki.

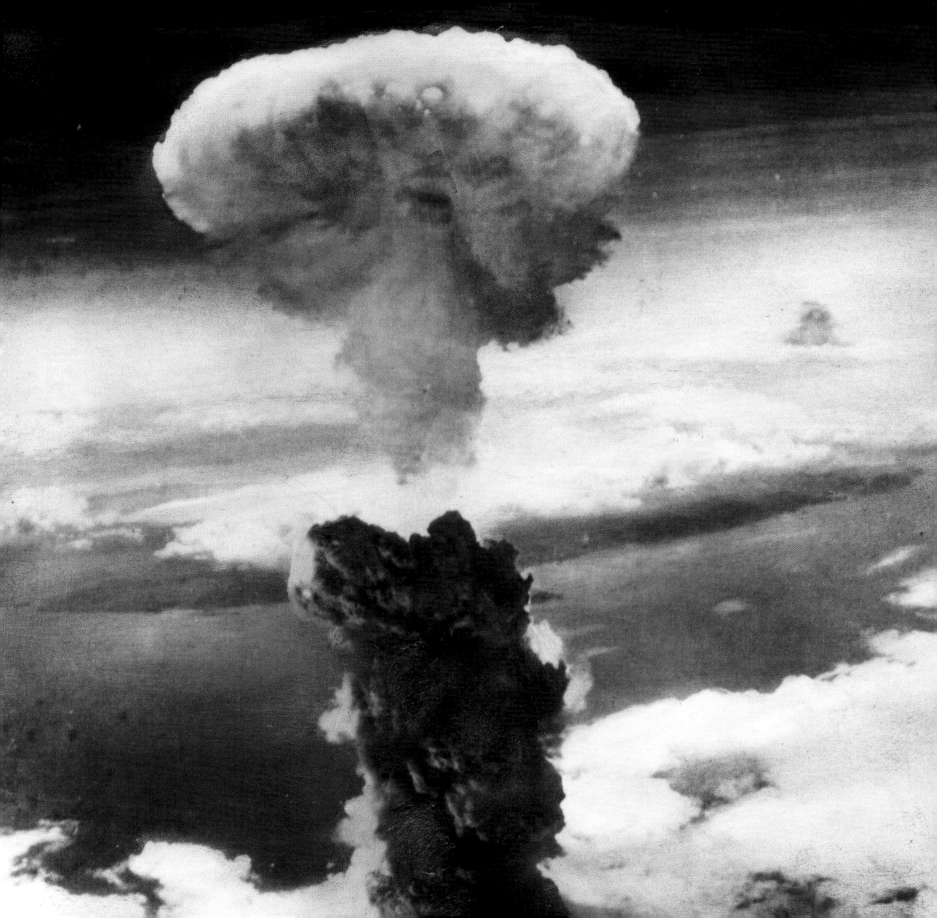

Above: Nagasaki after the atomic bomb attack; *right:* two survivors.
Opposite: A schoolboy survivor showing radiation burns.

QUICK FACTS

⭐ V-J (Victory in Japan) Day is celebrated on August 15th, the day Japan announced its surrender.

⭐ The U.S. flag flying over the *Missouri* was the same one that had flown over the Capitol on December 7, 1941, the day of the Japanese attack on Pearl Harbor.

⭐ There were 2 copies of the surrender document: The Allies' copy was bound in leather. Japan's copy was bound in canvas.

⭐ The Japanese delegate was so distraught that he had to be shown where to sign on the surrender document.

⭐ American troops had already landed in Japan and were taking control before the surrender ceremony.

⭐ Gen. MacArthur was appointed Supreme Commander, Allied Powers and would be the new military governor of Japan.

Above: Victorious soldiers returning to American soil. *Opposite:* Gen. Douglas MacArthur signs the Japanese surrender treaty on the battleship USS *Missouri.*

On September 2, 1945 at 9 A.M. on the deck of the battleship USS *Missouri,* the Japanese signed the documents of surrender. World War II was finally over. Servicemen all over the world could finally go home.

The best moment of the war for millions of American servicemen was when they disembarked from their ships onto American soil. The war was over and they were still alive and had come home. Not many had expected to make it. Those who managed to live through the conflict in Europe and those still alive in the Pacific had been convinced that their next mission would be the invasion of Japan, where casualties numbering in the hundreds of thousands were expected. Men who later got an eighty to ninety-five percent disability from the government had been listed as fit for combat for Japan.

But with the atomic bomb and Japan's surrender, everything changed. Suddenly the servicemen could think about returning to the States and the joy of reuniting with their loved ones, going to college or getting a job, getting married, and raising a family. These men, and the millions of others like them, got on with their lives. They went out and built modern America —the Interstate highways, the St. Lawrence Seaway, the suburbs, the modern corporation, tens of thousands of small businesses, the computer, the revolutions in communications, agriculture, education, medicine and more. They helped eliminate segregation, which brought African-Americans, Spanish-speaking Americans, Asian Americans, and women into the mainstream of American life. They changed this country and the world.

Above: Celebrating V-J Day in New York City's Times Square.

QUICK FACTS

⭐ The International Military Tribunal that oversaw the trial in Nuremberg had one judge each from Great Britain, the United States, the Soviet Union and France.

⭐ The high Nazi official Martin Bormann was sentenced to death in absentia because he had not been captured. His body was later discovered in Berlin during excavation at a construction site. Apparently he had been killed while trying to escape before the Russian Army captured Berlin.

⭐ The trials established a new kind of judgment on the behavior of a nation's leaders and created a new type of crime for which the accused could be punished, crimes against humanity.

⭐ Normally a person cannot be tried for something he or she did before a law was created to prohibit it. The war crimes trials were controversial because of their ex post facto—retroactive—application of the new law prohibiting crimes against humanity.

A s the war was ending the Allies appointed an International War Crimes Commission to gather evidence against the Nazi and Japanese leaders who had violated the rules of war agreed to under the Geneva Convention and who had committed crimes against humanity.

Twenty-two Nazi leaders in Nuremberg, Germany, and twenty-five Japanese war leaders in Tokyo, Japan, were brought to trial.

For the Nazis, the charges included using slave labor and being partners in Hitler's Final Solution (the Holocaust). For the Japanese leaders, the charges included breaching the laws and customs of war and allowing atrocities to be committed by their Army and Navy.

Of the Nazis, twelve were condemned to death, seven were given prison terms and three were set free. Of the Japanese, all were found guilty, and seven were given the death sentence.

Albert Speer, the Minister of Armaments and War Production for Nazi Germany who received a twenty-year sentence at Spandau Prison, said, "The trial is necessary. There is a shared responsibility for such horrible crimes even in an authoritarian state."

Right: General Hideki Tojo, flanked by uniformed guards, at his war crimes trial in Tokyo, Japan.
Opposite: Nazi leaders at their war crimes trial in Nuremberg, Germany. (Top row, left to right: Baldur von Schirach, Fritz Sauckel, Alfred Jodl; bottom row, left to right: Hermann Göring, Rudolf Hess, Joachim von Ribbentrop, Wilhelm Keitel, Ernst Kaltenbrunner.)

QUICK FACTS

★ From 1948–1952, the Marshall Plan contributed $13,015,000,000 to European recovery.

★ 10,000 workers in Birmingham, England had jobs again thanks to Marshall Plan shipments of carbon black, a substance used to make tires.

★ American experts showed Dutch soap makers how to cut down soap making time from 5 days to 2 hours.

★ American 4-H Club members sent 1,000 baby chicks to children in Vienna, Austria.

★ Japan received aid through the U.S. government's Mutual Security Agency and other economic programs.

It was 1947. World War II had been over for two years. But the countries in Europe were still in ruins. Their governments needed help rebuilding everything the war had destroyed—cities, roads, and the lives of millions of people.

The United States, protected by two oceans, had not suffered the way Europe had. In fact, it was now the richest and strongest country in the world. President Truman and other leaders saw that they had to help. But they did not want to give the Europeans a credit card with no spending limit.

George Marshall was now the secretary of state. He was responsible for America's relations with foreign countries. In a graduation speech at Harvard University on June 5, 1947, he said that the United States was ready to help the Europeans. "Our policy . . . ," he declared, "is directed against hunger, poverty, desperation, and chaos." But the American government would not help on a piecemeal basis. It wished to work together to restore the war-torn countries. He ended his speech by saying, "The initiative, I think, must come from Europe." This marked the beginning of the Marshall Plan, the greatest foreign aid program ever.

The United States gave money, materials, and assistance of every kind to governments, businesses, industries, and individual people. All that the United States asked was that the help be put to good use. The grateful nations of Europe complied. Within a few short years countries that had been on the brink of chaos were robust and healthy. Former Prime Minister Winston Churchill described the Marshall Plan as "the most unsordid act in history."

Left: American coal being unloaded in Europe.
Opposite: Reconstruction in Berlin thanks to Marshall Plan aid.

GLOSSARY

Allies—The name for the nations, primarily Great Britain, the United States, the Soviet Union, and France, united against the Axis powers of Germany, Italy, and Japan.

Amphibious—Able to operate on land and water.

Armada—A large group of warships.

Atomic bomb—An explosive weapon made of either uranium or plutonium that gets its destructive power from the rapid release of nuclear energy.

Axis—Primarily the countries of Germany, Italy, and Japan that fought against the Allies.

Blitzkrieg—The German word for "lightning war." A swift, overpowering military offensive of combined land and air forces led by tanks and other armored vehicles.

Bombardier—A member of a military aircraft crew responsible for operating the bombing equipment.

Bunker—A defensive fortification that is a man-made hill of dirt and stone that hides and protects a cannon or machine gun and its crew.

Campaign—A series of major military operations designed to achieve a long-range goal.

Carbon black—The fine, sootlike material that results from the incomplete burning of natural gas or petroleum oil and is used primarily in rubber and ink.

Carrier borne airplanes—Military aircrafts designed to be launched and retrieved on warships that have large, flat, runway-shaped decks (aircraft carriers).

Chancellor—The supreme appointed political official, usually in Europe, similar in power and authority to the president of the United States.

Communism—A social system created by Karl Marx characterized by a classless society and the absence of private property ownership.

Communist Revolution—The overthrow, usually by violent means, of a nation's government by the political party whose members follow the beliefs of Karl Marx.

Concentration camps—A fenced and guarded group of buildings designed to hold political prisoners and/or prisoners of war.

Coolie—A derogatory term for an unskilled Chinese laborer.

Corpsman—An enlisted soldier or sailor trained to provide medical assistance, usually on the battlefield.

Cremation—The burning of a dead body until it is transformed into ashes.

Crimes against humanity—Extreme, unlawful acts committed against population centers or ethnic groups.

Death in Absentia—A sentence of execution delivered to a criminal defendant who does not attend his trial.

D-Day—Literally "Day-Day." Originally the codename for the day on which a military offensive is to be launched. Specifically refers to June 6, 1944, the Allied invasion of Normandy, France.

Democracy—Government by the people exercised either directly or through elected representatives.

Distinguished Service Cross—The U.S. Army medal awarded for exceptional heroism in combat. It is the second highest award for bravery after the Medal of Honor.

Dive-bomber—Warplane that attacks its target by flying toward it at a steep angle prior to the release of its explosives.

Embrasure—An opening in the wall of a bunker or pillbox for a cannon or a machine gun.

Escort—One or more vehicles, aircrafts, or ships charged with accompanying another in order to guide or protect it. Destroyer escorts and escort carriers are smaller versions of the standard-sized destroyers and aircraft carriers.

Espionage—The act or practice of spying on others, especially countries.

Ex post facto—In law, penalties enacted, often months or years later, against individuals who committed the acts before they were judged crimes.

Final Solution—German Chancellor Adolf Hitler's program for the systematic killing of the Jewish race.

Frontline—the border between two opposing armies.

Führer—The German word for "leader." The title that Hitler assumed for himself once he obtained dictatorial powers after he became Chancellor.

Garrison—A military post or a group of troops stationed at a particular location.

Gassed—The use of highly toxic fumes in an enclosed space by concentration camp officials to kill inmates. It was one of the methods used in the Final Solution.

Geneva Convention—One of several international agreements that regulates the treatment and rights of wounded combatants and prisoners of war.

Gestapo—The Nazi-organized German internal security police. Short for GEheime STaatsPOlizei (secret state police).

GI—Nickname for a U.S. soldier. It is the abbreviation for "Government Issue."

Internment—The detaining or confining of individuals in wartime. Usually done by a neutral country when combatants enter its territorial boundary.

Island Hopping Campaign—A series of offensive military operations designed to neutralize enemy-held islands through the act of bypassing them and seizing nearby and lightly defended islands.

Isolationists—Those who advocate that their country remain aloof from political or economic relationships with other countries, especially ones at war.

GLOSSARY

Kamikaze—The Japanese word for "divine wind." In World War II, kamikaze were Japanese pilots trained to make suicide attacks on enemy targets, usually warships, with their warplanes.

Kristallnacht—In German, "The Night of Broken Glass." The night of Nazi-organized looting and burning of Jewish homes and stores on November 9–10, 1938.

Landing Vehicle Tanks—One of a group of specially designed flat-bottomed transport vessels. Landing Vehicle Tanks were used to carry armored vehicles and deliver them directly onto a beach.

Lebensraum—The German word for "living room." The term used by the Nazis as a slogan for German expansionism, particularly eastward.

Luftwaffe—The German Air Force.

Medal of Honor—The highest military decoration awarded in the United States to all branches for gallantry and bravery above and beyond the call of duty in action against the enemy.

Mein Kampf—*My Struggle*. Adolf Hitler's book that was both his autobiography and a statement of his political beliefs and plans.

Merchant ships—Vessels designed to transport supplies and goods.

Military zones—Areas of a country where civilians are governed by administrators from the armed forces.

Nazi—The acronym for NAtionalsoZIalist, the first word of the official title of Hitler's political party, the Nationalsozialistische Deutsche Arbeiterpartie or NSDAP (National Socialist German Worker's Party).

Nisei—Native born, second generation Japanese-American citizens.

Nuremberg Racial Laws—Decrees enacted by the Nazis that stripped German Jews of their citizenship, prohibited them from marrying non-Jews, and prevented them from working as servants in non-Jewish German homes.

Panzer—The German term for "armor." In World War II *Panzerwagen*, or tank, was shortened to Panzer.

Pillbox—A roofed concrete defensive fortification designed to hold a machine gun or cannon and its crew.

Plutonium—A highly toxic radioactive metal used in making the atomic bomb.

Pogrom—An organized and officially sanctioned persecution or massacre of an ethnic group, especially Jews.

Policy of Appeasement—The granting of concessions by a government to a potential enemy in order to maintain peaceful international relations.

Pontoon—A flat-bottomed boat or other structure used to support a floating bridge.

POW—Prisoner of War. Combatants captured by opposing forces and confined to special compounds, either concentration camps or prisoner of war camps.

Purple Heart—U.S. military decoration awarded in all branches and all ranks to members who are wounded in combat action.

Sabotage—The damage of property or actions of a country by enemy spies.

Seppuku—Japanese for "honorable suicide." The Japanese suicide ritual using a knife to cut open the abdomen.

SONAR—Acronym for SOund NAvigation Ranging. An electronic device used by ships to detect submarines.

Soviet Union—From 1917–1991, the nation known officially as the Union of Soviet Socialist Republics; a nation containing 15 Communist-governed republics and dominated by its largest republic, Russia.

Strafing—The attack with machine-gun fire from low-flying warplanes.

Theater—The large geographical area where military operations are coordinated.

Trade embargo—The policy of a nation to refuse to conduct economic relations with another country.

Treaty—A formal agreement between two or more nations that contains terms of trade, military alliance, or other points of mutual interest.

Tribunal—A court of justice.

Tripartite Pact—The treaty between Germany, Italy, and Japan intended to provide mutual assistance in the event of an attack on any of them by the United States.

Tundra—In the arctic regions, the treeless area between the ice cap and the treeline.

Turkey shoot—Term for the competitive hunting of a game bird. In World War II, the description of the overwhelming destruction of the Japanese Navy warplanes with almost no losses by the U.S. Naval Air Force during the Battle of the Philippine Sea.

U-boat—Abbreviation for the German term *"Unterseeboot"* (underwater boat). The name commonly given to German submarines.

Uranium—A silvery, radioactive metal that, like plutonium, is the explosive element in an atomic bomb.

V-E Day—Victory in Europe Day. The day when representatives of the German government signed the surrender agreement on May 7, 1945, ending the war in Europe and subsequently celebrated each year on that day.

V-J Day—Victory in Japan Day. The day Japan accepted terms for unconditional surrender from Allies, August 15, 1945, ending the war with Japan and concluding World War II.

Williwaw—A violent gust of cold wind blowing seaward from the mountain coast.

BIBLIOGRAPHY

Ambrose, Stephen E. 1997. *Citizen Soldiers.* Simon & Schuster.
——. 1994. *D-Day June 6, 1944: The Climactic Battle of World War II.* Simon & Schuster.
——. 1998. *The Victors.* Simon & Schuster.
Ambrose, Stephen E. and C. L. Sulzberger. 1997. *American Heritage New History of World War II.* Viking.
Baldwin, Hanson W. 1966. *Battles Lost and Won.* Konecky & Konecky.
Blumenson, Martin. 1974. *The Patton Papers 1940–1945.* Da Capo Press.
Boatner II, Mark M. 1996. *The Biographical Dictionary of World War II.* Presidio Press.
Collins, Larry and Dominique Lapierre. 1965. *Is Paris Burning?* Simon & Schuster.
Dear, I. C. B. and M. R. D. Foot, editors. 1995. *The Oxford Companion to World War II.* Oxford University Press.
D'Este, Carlo. 1995. *Patton: A Genius for War.* HarperCollins.
Eisenhower, David. 1986. *Eisenhower at War 1943-1945.* Random House.
Garfield, Brian. 1982. *The Thousand-Mile War.* Bantam Books.
Hoyt, Edwin P. 1999. *Guadalcanal.* Scarborough House.
Jablonski, Edward. 1971. *Airwar.* Doubleday & Company.
Keegan, John. 1989. *The Second World War.* Penguin Books.
Lord, Walter. 1957. *Day of Infamy.* Henry Holt and Company.
——. 1967. *Incredible Victory.* Harper & Row.
Love, Robert W. Jr. 1992. *History of the U.S. Navy Volume Two 1942–1991.* Stackpole Books.
Manchester, William. 1978. *American Caesar.* Laurel.
——. June 14, 1987. "The Bloodiest Battle of All." *The New York Times Magazine.*
——. 1980. *Goodbye, Darkness.* Laurel.
Mee, Charles L., Jr. 1984. *The Marshall Plan.* Simon & Schuster.
Mosley, Leonard. 1982. *Marshall Hero for Our Times.* Hearst Books.
Natkiel, Richard. 1985. *Atlas of World War II.* The Military Press.
Payne, Robert. 1966. *The Horizon Book of Ancient Rome.* American Heritage Publishing Co., Inc.
Persico, Joseph E. 1994. *Nuremberg Infamy on Trial.* Penguin Books.
Phillips, Cabell. 1966. *The Truman Presidency.* The MacMillan Company.
Pimlott, John. 1995. *The Historical Atlas of World War II.* Henry Holt and Company.
Porges, Irwin. 1975. *Edgar Rice Burrough: The Man Who Created Tarzan.* Brigham Young University Press.
Reisner, Marc. 1986. *Cadillac Desert.* Viking Penguin, Inc.
Snyder, Louis L. 1982. *Louis L. Snyder's Historical Guide to World War II.* Greenwood Press.
Speer, Albert. 1970. *Inside the Third Reich.* The Macmillan Company.
Stafford, Commander Edward P. 1962. *The Big E: The Story of the USS Enterprise.* Ballantine Books.
Stewart, Adrian. 1979. *The Battle of Leyte Gulf.* Robert Hale.
Sweeney, Major General Charles W., U.S.A.F. (Ret.) with James A. Antonucci and Marion K. Antonucci. 1997. *War's End.* Avon Books.
Wallechinsky, David and Irving Wallace, editors. 1975. *The People's Almanac.* Doubleday & Company.

RELATED WEB SITES

The Air Force Historical Research Agency
www.au.af.mil/au/afhra/

The Congressional Medal of Honor Society
www.cmohs.org/society.htm

The Eisenhower Center for American Studies
www.uno.edu/~eice

E. Stanley Wright Museum: America at War 1939–1945: The Home Front
www.wrightmuseum.org

The Higgins Boat Project
www.higginsboat.org

National Archives and Records Administration
www.nara.gov

National D-Day Museum
www.ddaymuseum.org

The Naval Historical Center
www.history.navy.mil/

Simon Wiesenthal Center Multimedia Learning Center Online
http://motlc.wiesenthal.com

U.S. Army Center of Military History
www2.army.mil/cmh-pg/

United States Holocaust Memorial Museum
www.ushmm.org

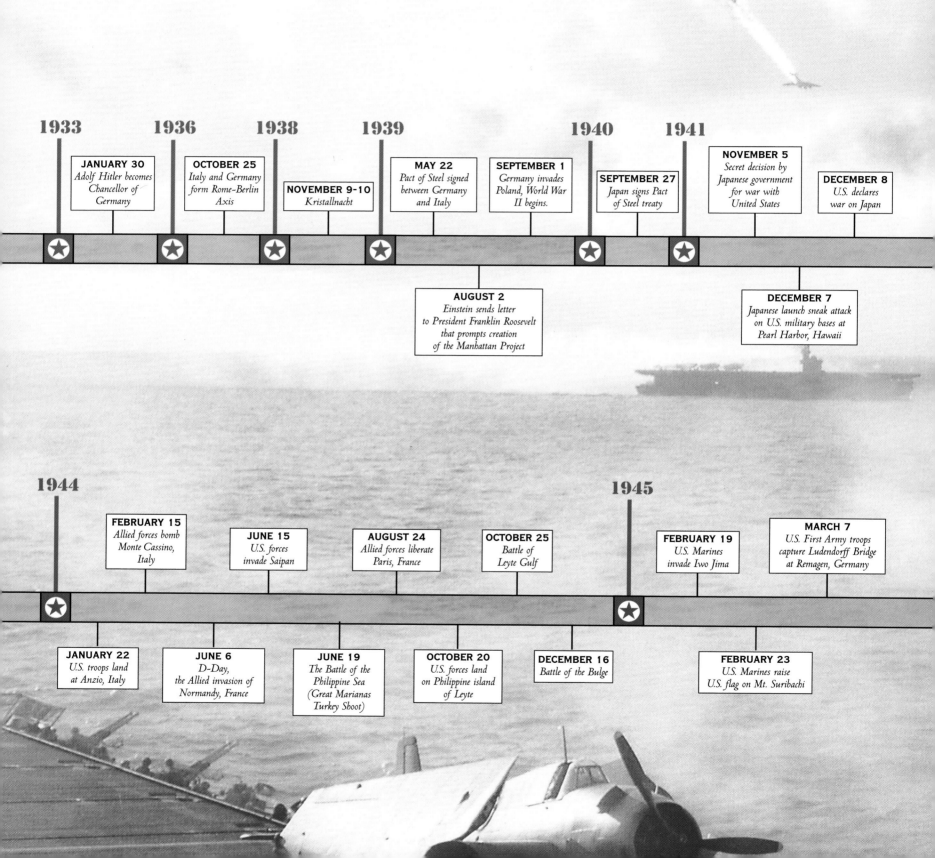

1933

JANUARY 30
Adolf Hitler becomes Chancellor of Germany

1936

OCTOBER 25
Italy and Germany form Rome-Berlin Axis

1938

NOVEMBER 9-10
Kristallnacht

1939

MAY 22
Pact of Steel signed between Germany and Italy

SEPTEMBER 1
Germany invades Poland, World War II begins.

1940

SEPTEMBER 27
Japan signs Pact of Steel treaty

1941

NOVEMBER 5
Secret decision by Japanese government for war with United States

DECEMBER 8
U.S. declares war on Japan

AUGUST 2
Einstein sends letter to President Franklin Roosevelt that prompts creation of the Manhattan Project

DECEMBER 7
Japanese launch sneak attack on U.S. military bases at Pearl Harbor, Hawaii

1944

FEBRUARY 15
Allied forces bomb Monte Cassino, Italy

JUNE 15
U.S. forces invade Saipan

AUGUST 24
Allied forces liberate Paris, France

OCTOBER 25
Battle of Leyte Gulf

1945

FEBRUARY 19
U.S. Marines invade Iwo Jima

MARCH 7
U.S. First Army troops capture Ludendorff Bridge at Remagen, Germany

JANUARY 22
U.S. troops land at Anzio, Italy

JUNE 6
D-Day, the Allied invasion of Normandy, France

JUNE 19
The Battle of the Philippine Sea (Great Marianas Turkey Shoot)

OCTOBER 20
U.S. forces land on Philippine island of Leyte

DECEMBER 16
Battle of the Bulge

FEBRUARY 23
U.S. Marines raise U.S. flag on Mt. Suribachi